50 BEST SCRAMBLES

in the

Lake District

(Right) Scrambling through the rocky pinnacles on
Striding Edge
(Overleaf) On the summit of Blencathra

50 Best Scrambles
in the
Lake District
Bill O'Connor

David & Charles

A DAVID & CHARLES BOOK

Copyright © Bill O'Connor, 1995
Maps by Al Phizacklea
First published 1995
Published in paperback 1997

ISBN 0 7153 0697 9

Typeset by Blanc Verso
and printed in Italy by Milanostampa SpA
for David & Charles
Brunel House Newton Abbot Devon

Jacket photographs: (front) *Striding Edge,
Helvellyn;* (back) *Scramble A, Brim Fell: a
fantastic position above Low Water
overlooking Coniston*

CONTENTS

Introduction 6

What Is Scrambling? 6

The Scrambler's Habitat 10

Clothing and Equipment 10

A Code for Scramblers 12

How to use this book 12

Maps and Diagrams 16

Grades 16

Graded List of Scrambles 16–17

Quality 18

Navigation 18

THE FIRST SCRAMBLE 19

1 Broad Stand: A poet's corner
on Scafell 20

NORTH-WESTERN FELLS 23

2 Ashness Gill and a round of High
Seat, Shivery Man and Blea Tarn 24

3 Nitting Haws, Tiggywinkle
and Little Town 27

4 The Gables via Sourmilk Gill
and Rabbit's Trod 30

5 Combe Gill: Intake Ridge and
Attic Cave on Dovenest Crag 35

6 Cam Crag Ridge, Langstrath 38

7 Head of Newlands: Lowthwaite
Crag and Dale Head Pillar 41

8 Honister Crag and the delights
of Hay Stacks and High Stile 45

9 Grey Crag by way of Harrow
Buttress and Chockstone Ridge,
Birkness Combe 50

10 Lorton Gully, Grasmoor, and a
round of Hopegill Head and
Whiteside 54

11 Launchy Gill, Thirlmere, with
Dob Gill and a round of tarns 58

12 Pillar Rock by the Slab and
Notch route   62

NORTH-EASTERN FELLS   **65**

13 Fairfield by way of Link Cove
Gill and Greenhow End Slabs   66

14 Mill Gill and the Dodds,
St John's in the Vale   70

15 Helvellyn Gill and Browncove
Crags   74

16 Blencathra: Sharp Edge and
Hall's Fell Ridge   77

17 Mosedale Beck Force, Swindale   *81*

18 Hopgill Beck and
Rowantreethwaite Gill, Mardale   *84*

19 Blea Water Crag Gill to High
Street and Long Stile Ridge   *87*

20 Pinnacle Ridge, St Sunday
Crag   *90*

21 Helvellyn's Horseshoe:
Striding Edge and Swirral Edge   *94*

SOUTH-WESTERN FELLS   **97**

22 Low-level scrambles around
Wasdale: Pike Crag, Iron Crag,
Nether Beck Gorge, Bowderdale
Boulder and Bell Rib   *98*

23 South-east face of Ill Crag,
Eskdale, and the highest
summit in England   *102*

24 Ill Gill, Kirk Fell and the
Mosedale skyline with Nether
Beck Gorge   *105*

25 Gable: Napes Needle, Eagle's Nest
Gully, Arrowhead Ridge and
Westmorland Crag   *108*

26 Esk Gorge and Cam Spout
to Mickledore and Scafell   *114*

27 Tarn Beck, Great Blake Rigg
and a round of Seathwaite Tarn   *118*

28 Main face of Pike o' Stickle
and the Langdale skyline   *121*

29 Dungeon Ghyll, Harrison
Stickle and Jack's Rake   *124*

30 Great Carrs Buttress with
Swirl How and Wetherlam or
Tilberthwaite Gill   *128*

31 Low Water Beck, Brim Fell
and Coniston Fells   *132*

32 Dow: F Buttress and
B Buttress   *136*

33 Belles Knot, the Easedale
Matterhorn, by way of
Sourmilk and Easedale Gills   *139*

Acknowledgements   **142**

Index   **143**

INTRODUCTION

My lifelong love affair with the Lake District's mountains began when I learned to climb on its crags more than 30 years ago. I was fortunate to be introduced to them by people with a passion for steep places, high camps and long walks on lonely fells. It was a perfect beginning to my mountaineering apprenticeship. As an enthusiastic youngster I soon aspired to greater things – the climbs on Gable, Scafell and Pillar – and was impressed and influenced by the pioneers of our sport who had practised their craft on lakeland crags. Many were famous mountaineers whose exploits ranged the world's mountains; others were local cragsmen who were connoisseurs of lakeland rock. All, without exception, had absorbed the beauty and uniqueness of Cumbria's mountains that has much to do with its special blend of light and landscape, a quality that painters and poets have for centuries tried to capture. For me it is totally beguiling. Having stolen my heart I have returned to live amongst its eastern fells in sight of High Street and Blencathra.

Much of what is special about the Lake District has to do with a history responsible for producing its rich and varied landscape. Wherever you walk or climb you uncover a colourful tapestry woven by ancient Britons, Celts, Romans, Vikings, Saxons and Normans and strongly influenced by the border Scots. On top of this is a layer of mountaineering history studded with the names of modernday heroes. Fortunately, the Lake District is not a museum but a living landscape which has been cultivated by the people who work the land, miners and farmers alike. Our national parks, unlike those in other parts of the world, are not owned by the state or set aside for recreational use. They are privately owned and support a working community. Those that live, work and play in them must share its heritage, mindful of each other's interests. We can play our part by leaving stones unturned and vegetation and wildlife undisturbed. The Sierra Club motto, 'take only photographs, leave only footprints' will leave the Lakes a delight for our children's children.

For many visitors to the Lake District it is the home of mint-cake, Peter Rabbit and *Swallows and Amazons*. For mountaineers it is the cradle of rock climbing, where the solo first ascent of Napes Needle in 1866 by Walter Parry Haskett-Smith is recognised as the birth of the sport in Britain. What few realise is that 'scrambling' for pleasure was also born on lakeland rock when, in 1802, the poet Samuel Taylor Coleridge climbed Scafell. Descending towards Mickledore late in the afternoon he made the first descent of Broad Stand, and wrote about the experience in a letter. For many years Broad Stand remained the hardest scramble in the land. Coleridge was not the only poet to understand the power and pleasure of steep places. William Wordsworth, the quintessential lakeland wordsmith, loved the fells and knew their ridges, tarns and gills intimately. It is obvious from his writing that he had experienced the exhilaration of scrambling at first hand. In 'The Prelude', perhaps his finest poem, he wrote:

Oh! when I have hung
Above the raven's nest, by knots of grass
And half-inch fissures in the slippery rock
But ill sustained, and almost, as it seemed
Suspended by the blast that blew amain,
Shouldering the naked crag; Oh! at that time,
While on the perilous ridge I hung alone...

This was the beginning of a fine pastime that grows richer to this day. The opportunity for scrambling in the Lake District seems inexhaustible, holding in store hidden places still unexplored or unrecorded. Much of the pleasure of scrambling in the Lakes can be found in its variety. For the adventurous scrambler there are sinuous ridges to traverse, broad buttresses to climb and thundering fern-filled gills to explore.

WHAT IS SCRAMBLING?

Scrambling is not an easy concept to define: I don't want to imply is that it is something separate, a craft or sport in its own right. I see scrambling as part of mountaineering along with hill walking, snow and ice climbing, rock climbing and indeed ski touring. In the end they are all integral parts of mountaineering; skills that, once learned, help us enjoy

Traversing Helm Crag high above Grasmere (see route 33)

mountains to the full. It might be helpful to try to define scrambling in terms of a 'mountaineering continuum'. At one end there is walking, pure and simple, at the other, the extreme end if you like, there is technical climbing on rock and ice. Somewhere in the middle of this imaginary progression is scrambling; it begins where walking ends and ends where rock climbing begins. The problem, as ever, is coming to an agreement about where these lines are to be drawn. If nothing else, the debate will help pass the odd evening in the Wasdale Head, Old Dungeon Ghyll or Golden Rule.

Shortly after I became gripped by a love of mountains I was given a book written by Edward Whymper – his classic *Scrambles Amongst the Alps 1860–69.* It had a big influence on me. Whymper orchestrated and took part in the first ascent of the Matterhorn in 1865, the year before Napes Needle was climbed! Today, many would argue that Whymper should have called his book *Climbs Amongst The Alps* and that his routes on the Matterhorn, Pelvoux or Grandes Jorasses are much too difficult or dangerous to be called scrambling, I don't agree. I believe and have always felt that rock scrambling offers the greatest freedom and sense of adventure. I also believe that it is potentially amongst the most committing and dangerous of the 'games climbers play' and therein lies much of its

Ill Gill, Kirk Fell and the fell of the Mosedale round seen from Great Gable

attraction. For that reason I prefer to think of scrambling as another way of enjoying the mountains, not as something 'more difficult than walking' or 'less skilful than rock climbing'. In that respect, the continuum concept does not work. As with many situations in mountaineering the perception of difficulty and danger is a personal thing. Experience, skill, fitness and conditions help us make judgements about 'what is acceptable risk' and 'what is not possible'.

Perhaps one of the most enjoyable elements of scrambling is continuous movement over awkward ground. Whereas walking is about putting one foot in front of another, scrambling makes us use our hands and feet, and, most important of all, our heads; not as another point of contact, you understand, but the brain must be engaged before you overcome an awkward step or find the best line up a complex buttress or avoid a soaking in a thundering gill. Scrambling can be totally satisfying because it engages brain and brawn.

Most people who enjoy the hills find scrambling quite natural. It is enjoyable hopping skilfully from boulder to boulder or playing amongst rocks. Frictioning up a rough slab can be pure sensory pleasure whilst pulling on 'jugs' up a steep wall is a primordial delight – both are essential skills in the scrambler's repertoire. Unlike the rock climber for whom the norm is ropes, being belayed and using all manner of protection, the scrambler usually climbs unroped. Even when climbing with

friends, the scrambler is to all intents and purposes soloing and the consequences of a fall are serious. Of course, there are times, on difficult scrambles or when conditions or companions demand, that a rope is called for and should be used. It is then that a scrambler must know all about rope work, belaying and protection, and how to abseil and retreat safely from unsafe places. In this respect, scrambling is no different from rock climbing and the degree of skill required is no less demanding.

This brings me back to Whymper's book and why I prefer his title. Let me explain. At the time when Whymper was climbing during the second half of the nineteenth century, Alpinists were making first ascents of mountains. Their aim was to find the easiest and safest way to their chosen summit – and down again! Equipment was basic and so were their techniques. Climbers invariably followed professional guides, most of the time moving together, often unroped. When roped, they climbed with only a short distance between them. On more difficult sections they found a safe stance and stopped to let the guide go ahead to find the route and belay. From his safe stance he then brought the party on with a rope from above. In those days they had a rule: 'the leader must not fall'. It seems to me that this is a perfect description of scrambling today, apart from the fact that most scramblers do not take a guide. Victorian mountaineers also had another rule. They did not climb up what they could not climb down. This makes absolute sense for the modern scrambler for whom abseiling and the use of the rope to safeguard descents is essential.

THE SCRAMBLER'S HABITAT

Unlike the rock climber who prefers pristine crags, sea cliffs, outcrops and, increasingly, indoor climbing walls, the scrambler has no such constrictions. One of the joys of the game is that it uses precisely the kinds of terrain most rock climbers avoid; the gullies, shattered buttresses, rocky ridges and gills, unique habitats that cannot be explored from the tourist track.

Many of the scrambles described in this book were first discovered by the pioneers of Cumbrian climbing. Today, with soaring standards, they barely find a mention in the climbing guides of the Fell and Rock Climbing Club. The Lake District has few long or sustained rock ridges if you compare it with Scotland. The best – Sharp Edge and Striding Edge – demand little more than walking. All the same, they are exposed and potentially dangerous, especially under wet, windy or wintery conditions. Helvellyn's ridges have few equals anywhere in Britain when it comes to accidents or underestimates of difficulty. On the other hand, buttresses abound in the Lakes. Not all are as continuous or long as those around Scafell or Coniston's fells but invariably outcrops and rocky steps can be combined to provide a challenging and interesting route to the tops. As well, there are plenty of gills. These steep watercourses that cut and cascade down the fellside, harbour the hidden treasure of lakeland scrambling. They are unique places, providing an unusual perspective of the fells that remains well hidden from the casual passer-by.

CLOTHING AND EQUIPMENT

There is no particular equipment or type of clothing for scramblers, no lycra tights or hi-tech gadgets. The scrambler simply has to make do with a combination of walking and climbing gear – in fact, it is back to basics!

The ideal clothing for scrambling provides comfort, which means the right gear for the conditions. I like to wear neat-fitting clothing that allows a wide range of movement without being tight. You do not want baggy clothing that gets in the way. By and large, scrambling is more dynamic than walking so you should have warm and wicking layers with adequate ventilation for the conditions you expect throughout the day. Be aware of the weather forecast and dress accordingly. On hot summer days in gills I prefer shorts and a T-shirt and often a lot less than that, especially if there is wading to do or waterfalls to climb.

Footwear

Footwear can be critical on difficult scrambles. Obviously, on mountain scrambles you want comfortable boots that will let you enjoy a long day's walk. However, you will benefit from having a slightly stiffer pair which will allow you to stand comfortably on smaller holds and edges. Modern lightweights like the Karrimor KSB are ideal for both scrambling and fell walking. Many scramblers enjoy climbing in specialist 'sticky rubber' rock boots – and why not? They are light and allow you to use the smallest holds and smears; they are a delight to climb in on all but greasy rock. Being tight-fitting they are impossible to walk far in and wear out quickly. On very greasy rock, especially in gills, a pair of old socks is ideal for scrambling. They act a bit like rope-soled boots favoured in the 1930s and if you have never climbed in socks you will be astonished at how effective they are on lichened rock. Other than that, many scramblers wear trainers.

Rope

Whether you use it or not you should always carry a rope when scrambling. Do not compromise and go for a short, thin, lightweight one. If you need to belay you need to do it properly – something which will become apparent if anyone falls off or you need to abseil. A full-weight or single rope is what you want, which means 10.5 or 11mm nylon which meets the UIAA specification. You will also need a couple of slings and karabiners and ideally a small selection of chocks. Unless I am doing a lot of roped scrambling I do not normally wear a harness but tie direct to the rope. For abseiling

A jigsaw puzzle of walled fields at the head of Wasdale seen from Gavel Neese

I use a long sling to form a seat harness. This is not as comfortable and is definitely a compromise in favour of weight.

Helmet
To wear one or not to wear one? Should you fall or have someone kick loose stones on your head you would undoubtedly say yes. Having said that, I do not normally wear one when scrambling and appreciate what can happen.

Rope Skills
As important as having all this stuff is knowing how to use it. Before you venture on to difficult ground practise the techniques of belaying, protection and abseiling somewhere where it is safe. Get sound instruction from a friend with experience or from a qualified British mountain guide. These skills will really give you the 'freedom of the hills'.

A CODE FOR SCRAMBLERS
Like any other user of the countryside, either at work or play, we have a responsibility to the environment and to others, including wildlife. We should aim to have minimum impact on the hills, disturbing the countryside as little as possible and respecting the rights of others. Obviously we need to observe the Country Code, making sure to close gates we open, not to climb or damage dry stone walls, leave litter or make a nuisance of ourselves. However, when scrambling we get very close to places few can visit. Sometimes this is a rare habitat for both flora and fauna so there are other considerations: take care not to pollute water sources, disturb nesting birds, remove plants or kick down loose rocks or roll boulders. Simply enjoy yourself and uphold the traditions, friendship and spirit of the hills that is the heritage of all mountaineers.

HOW TO USE THIS BOOK
Each chapter is based on what I regard as a good day on the hill and always includes a classic scramble, usually the best available from a particular starting point. Sometimes the day will include more than one scramble if it can be fitted logically into a particular round. Of course, you can simply opt to complete the scramble and return to the valley, but that option never seems to complete the day. Often more than one return route has been shown if there are good alternatives. All of the routes can be fitted comfortably into a reasonable day's effort, say 6 to 8 hours on average, although a few are shorter. Of course, there are some whippets about who could probably complete the lot in a long weekend – good luck to them.

Within each chapter I have tried to give you more than just dry route descriptions, offering instead information about local names, history

Left: Mill Gill. Steep climbing up the right wall avoids a wet line up the fall

Right: Descending Hall's Fell Ridge, Blencathra

*Left: Interesting
scrambling in Helvellyn
Gill*

*Right: A perfect evening
on the summit of
Blencathra, looking
towards the central fells*

and exploration. Of course, these can rarely be more than snippets but if they spur you on to find out more then I shall be pleased.

Maps and Diagrams

Traditional line maps have not been used, as they are not really useful for navigation. Instead, I have opted for Al Phizacklea's excellent perspective drawings, as they give a much better overall picture of the route and an idea of the 'shape' of the day. Each scramble relates to a particular OS Outdoor Leisure map of the English Lakes. Their scale is 1:25,000 and they are ideal for navigation. There are no routes that require more than one map. The Lam-Fold waterproof series are certainly worth the extra cost: they far outlast the standard map and do away with the need for a map case.

Grades

Just as rock climbs are graded for difficulty, so too are scrambles. Generally speaking, guidebooks have adopted three grades of difficulty for scrambles, and these have been used to grade the scrambles in this guide, along with a fourth for serious undertakings.

The following list provides the grade, area and chapter for each scramble. The grades are 1, 2, 3, and 3S (serious), and are explained below. A difficult route for the grade is shown by the addition of a ∗ in its grade box.

Grade 1

Grade 1 scrambles are fairly straightforward

Area	Scramble	Grade	Route
Blencathra	Hall's Fell Ridge	1	16
	Sharp Edge	1/2	16
Borrowdale	Nitting Haws	1/2	3
	Sourmilk Gill	1/2	4
	Dovenest Crag – Attic cave	2/3	5
	Intake Ridge	3	5
	Outake Ridge	3	5
	Ashness Gill	3s	5
Buttermere	Harrow Buttress	3	9
	Chockstone Ridge	3s	9
Coniston	Brim Fell	2	31
	Low Water Beck	3	31
	Dow B Buttress	3s	32
	Dow F Buttress	3s	32
Crummock	Lorton Gulley	3	10
Deepdale	Link Cove Gill	2/3	13
	Greenhow End Slabs	3	13
Duddon	Tarn Beck	1/2	27
	Great Blake Rigg	2/3	27
Easedale	Belles Knot	2	33
Eskdale	Esk Gorge	2/3	26
Gillercombe	Rabbit's Trod	3	4
Grasmere	Easedale Gill	1	33
	Sourmilk Gill – Easedale	1	33
Great Gable	Arrowhead Ridge	2	25
	Napes Needle	2	25
	Westmorland Crag	2	25
	Eagle's Nest Gully	2/3	25
Grisedale	Pinnacle Ridge	3	20
Helvellyn	Swirral Edge	.5	21
	Striding Edge	1	21

Area	Scramble	Grade	Route
Honister	Honister Crag	3s	8
Langdale	Dungeon Ghyll, Upper	1	29
	Jack's Rake	1	29
	Harrison Stickle – South-west face	2	29
	Pike o' Stickle – Face route	2	28
	Dungeon Ghyll, Lower	3	29
Langstrath	Cam Crag Ridge	2/3	6
Little Langdale	Tilberthwaite Gill	1/2	30
Mardale	Hopgill Beck	2	18
	Blea Water Crag Gill	3	19
	Rowantreethwaite Gill	3	18
Newlands	Dale Head Pillar	1	7
	Lowthwaite Crag	1/2	7
Pillar Rock	Slab and Notch	3s	12
Scafell	Broad Stand	3	1
St John's in the Vale	Mill Gill	3s	14
Swindale	Mosedale Beck Force	2/3	17
Thirlmere	Dob Gill	1	11
	Helvellyn Gill	1/2	15
	Browncave Crags	2/3	15
	Launchy Gill	3s	11
Upper Eskdale	Cam Spout	2/3	26
	Ill Crag – Eskdale	3	23
Wasdale	Bowderdale Boulder	–	22
	Iron Crag – Middle Fell	2	22
	Nether Beck Gorge	2	22, 24
	Pike Crag – Buckbarrow	2	22
	Bell Rib – Yewbarrow	2/3	22
	Ill Gill – Kirk Fell	3s	25
Weatherlam	Great Carrs Buttress	2	30

rough or exposed walks, with some difficult steps where you need to use hands and feet. Route finding is usually obvious, with considerable choice. Ropes are not usually required and escape or retreat is invariably easy.

Grade 2
Things are getting harder; the scrambling is more difficult and continuous. A rope may be required and route finding becomes more important if you are to find the best line. Escape becomes more difficult.

Grade 3
A combination of exposure, increased difficulty and route finding make this the hardest scrambling grade. These are usually more sustained than grade 2 routes. A rope is advisable even for rock climbers and escape or retreat becomes even more difficult.

Routes graded **3S** (marked with an asterisk in the box which grades each scramble) have all the difficulty associated with a grade 3 route but are also *serious* undertakings. This is usually because they are exposed or more sustained and escape is unusually difficult. These are still not as technically difficult or sustained as true rock climbs. Having said that, many scrambles have individual moves that are far harder than 'moderate' rock climbs. Indeed, you will find problems on scrambles – especially in gills where difficult moves have to be made on lichened rock – that, high above the ground, would become 'severe', extremely so!

It should be obvious that all these grades can be affected adversely by weather conditions. Strong winds on exposed ridges, heavy rain in a gill bed or both on a greasy buttress may make them unpleasant or impossible. But judge-ment is part of any climber's skill; it comes with experience, which, once gained, brings pleasure.

In wintery conditions most scrambles become very serious undertakings. Watercourses freeze up to form steep ice climbs, cornices form on ridges and buttresses under snow and ice can provide the most difficult and serious undertaking of all. In this case they require other skills and equipment and can no longer be considered scrambles.

QUALITY

All of the scrambles and walks in this book are amongst the most enjoyable in the Lake District and are worthy of three stars. That said I've tried to indicate their quality, one against another in the context of this book. Through a combination of position, rock quality, terrain and vegetation I find these more satisfying than others. See what you think.

NAVIGATION

As well as a technical guide for the scramble I have also indicated, on a scale of 1–3, the overall difficulty of finding your way to and from the scramble in poor conditions using a map and compass:

1 Straightforward
2 Appreciable accuracy required
3 Difficult

My assessment is highly subjective and your success in poor conditions will depend on yourskill, persistence and perhaps a little luck. In good weather you should have no problem with route finding. If you do I can only suggest that you spend some time practising the fundamentals of map and compass work.

Edward Whymper, after a lifetime of adventure and scrambling, died of old age in Chamonix at the foot of the mountains he loved. Here is some advice from him taken from *Scrambles Amongst The Alps 1860–69*.

There have been joys too great to be described in words, and there have been griefs upon which I have dared not dwell; and with these in mind I say, Climb if you will, but remember that courage and strength are nought without prudence, and that a momentary negligence may destroy the happiness of a lifetime. Do nothing in haste; look well to each step: and from the beginning think what may be the end.

Broad Stand on Scafell: the first recorded scramble in the Lake District

THE FIRST SCRAMBLE

Route 1: BROAD STAND: A POET'S CORNER ON SCAFELL

	1	2	3
grade			
quality			
navigation			

ASSESSMENT: A short, sharp scramble that was the first recorded rock climb in Britain; a milestone in mountaineering history.

Grade Note: Best combined with any scramble that takes you close to Mickledore or Scafell
GR: 210068
OS MAP: Outdoor Leisure 6

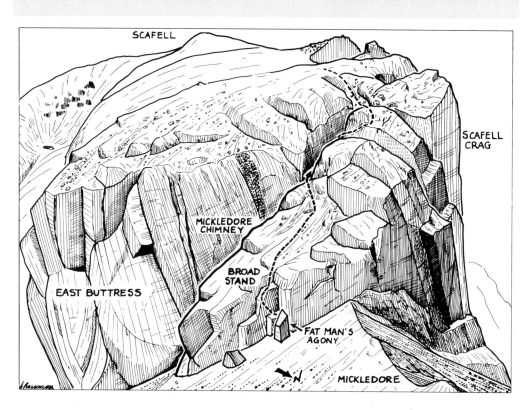

SCAFELL
SCAFELL CRAG
MICKLEDORE CHIMNEY
BROAD STAND
EAST BUTTRESS
FAT MAN'S AGONY
N
MICKLEDORE

Of all the scrambles on Lake District fells, Broad Stand must surely take pride of place. This is not because it is long or over difficult but because it represents a double first in the history of British mountaineering.

Broad Stand is high on Scafell; in fact it is almost the highest scramble in England. If you leave the summit of Scafell Pike and descend to Mickledore, the direct way to the summit of Scafell is barred by a barrier of crags that at first glance have few weaknesses and no walking route. On either side of the pass the ground drops steeply and Mountain Rescue Kit stowed nearby is a keen reminder to take care.

To the right the well worn path descends towards Wasdale where it is overshadowed by the awesome bulk of Scafell Crag, the finest in England, where many of our best rock climbs are found. For those with an interest in the sport, the great sweep of the Central Buttress will command your attention as it did those two great lakeland pioneers S.W. Herford and G.S. Sansom. This huge, smooth buttress has an obvious natural weakness in the form of a hanging flake in the centre of the face, with a crack below and not much above. In 1914, towards the end of April, Herford and Sansom set out to overcome the Central Buttress by the Flake Crack with two other climbers, Murray and Gibson. Over a number of days Herford and Sansom alone overcame the flake by forming a rope cradle around a chockstone to provide a belay. The leader then climbed onto the shoulders of his securely anchored second and reached the top of the flake. Their ascent is a real milestone in the history of lakeland climbing and it was not until 1931 that an ascent of CB, without the cradle and combined tactics, was done by that great and tragic climber, John Menlove Edwards. Tragically, in the summer of 1994 the vital chockstone was pulled from CB with fatal consequences.

But long before CB or even rock scrambling as a sport was established, Scafell was the scene for another milestone. The Lake District has always been the home of hardy people. They have had to be at ease on the fells tending sheep, mining minerals and building endless miles of monumental dry stone walls. It is likely that in the course of their labours they would have scrambled up steep rocks from time to time in the pursuit of sheep, minerals or eagles' eggs. Yet alas their efforts went unrecorded, which brings me back to Broad Stand and its double first and why it has pride of place in this book of classic lakeland scrambles.

In August 1802, the poet Samuel Taylor Coleridge set out on a 9 day walking tour, or what he called his 'circumcursion', of the Lake District. In itself it was a bold step to set off in wild country with little more than a scribbled sketch map. But to venture to the highest summits and even rock climb was a brilliant folly, for Coleridge, a friend of Wordsworth, was troubled in both mind and body. He was far from well physically, his marriage was falling apart, he was in love with another woman and was addicted to opium; not the ideal candidate

Climbing the crux of Broad Stand

for an outward bound course. But in Nature the poet sought solitude. For him, going alone was essential to the experience if he was to 'enrich his Imagination or Heart'.

During this pilgrimage Coleridge hiked to the summit of Scafell. Although dawning as a glorious day, by the time he set off the sky was full of ominous storm clouds. His map had no detail and he descended directly towards Mickledore. From above, this way appears obvious as it leads towards the Pikes and seems to offer the shortest descent to the hawse. At first all went well. The ground is easy enough and the rocks none too steep. Even where the route becomes more difficult the sight of easy ground not far below is most enticing. From above, the first of several wide rock ledges appear to be readily accessible and therein lay the trap and an experience which Coleridge recorded soon afterwards.

The first place I came to was not direct rock, I slipped down and went on for a while with tolerable ease – but now I came to a smooth perpendicular rock about 7 feet high – this was nothing – I put my hands on the ledge and dropped down – in a few yards came to such another – I dropped that too – and yet another seemed not higher – I would not stand for a trifle so I dropped that too – but the stretching of the muscles of my hands and arms, and the jolt of the Fall on my Feet, put my whole Limbs in a Tremble, and I paused, and looking down, saw that I had little else to encounter but a succession of these little Precipices... so I began to suspect that I ought not to go on, but then unfortunately tho' I could with ease drop down a smooth Rock 7 feet high, I could not climb it, so go on I must and on I went – the next three drops were not half a Foot, at least not a foot more than my own height, but every Drop increased the Palsy of my Limbs – I shook all over, heaven knows without the least influence of Fear – and now I only had two more to drop down, to return was impossible – but of these two the first was tremendous, it was twice my own height, and the Ledge at the bottom was so exceedingly narrow, that if I dropped down upon it I must

of necessity have fallen backwards and of course killed myself...
He thought for a while, weighed the risk and went for it. He succeeded: he wrote

I lay upon my back to rest myself, and was beginning... to laugh at myself for a madman, when the sight of the crags above me... overawed me. I lay in a state of almost prophetic Trance and Delight…

Later in the day he sheltered from a storm, with adrenaline surging he recorded feelings that many of us on Monday morning, back at work after a great weekend, have shared: 'O God! what thoughts were mine, O how I wished… that I might wander about for a Month… among these places so lonely and savage and full of sounds!'
All this was in a letter to Sara Hutchinson, the woman Coleridge loved, where he told her just how much his scrambling had enriched his 'Imagination and Heart' and left us with a double first: the first descent of Broad Stand and the first piece of writing that really captures the essence of our sport and the feelings that all of us experience sooner or later in our scrambling career .
Today, a descent of Broad Stand remains a bold step. Ascent, however, seems less forbidding but quite difficult none the less, and in wet conditions a rope is a sensible precaution. Plenty of would-be 'tigers' have suffered the same 'Palsy' of 'Limbs' on Broad

Stand that afflicted poor Coleridge. To walk to Mickledore just to scramble up Broad Stand is almost like a pilgrimage, but it can be done quite naturally in the course of a more ambitious day, say on Cam Spout or Ill Crag.
From Mickledore descend about 25m down scree towards Eskdale where the rock is split by a deep cleft, which is quite narrow. Coleridge wrote that from this ledge the rock was 'rent from top to bottom,' and that he 'slipped down as between two walls, without any danger or difficulty'. Having squeezed through the rent (Fat Man's Agony) you are faced with a corner on the left; in wet conditions this can be difficult. Climb it, making use of a crack and reach a larger ledge on which Coleridge must have dropped, lain on his back and looked up at the crags and swirling clouds.
Above you is a steep wall about 2.8m (9ft) high (which means Coleridge was 4ft 6in or making use of poetic licence). Climb this either in the corner or on good holds on the wall to the left. Above are a series of easier ledges which lead to scree and a well marked track that follows a ridge taking you past Pisgah, Scafell Pinnacle and Deep Gill. It remains a great way to the summit, despite being quite short. The alternatives to Scafell's summit are much longer and require you to descend from Mickledore and make a major detour around the crags of Scafell, either to Lord's Rake or Foxes Tarn.

Looking down on the sunlit hamlet of Grange-in-Borrowdale from Nitting Haws

NORTH-WESTERN FELLS

Route 2: Ashness Gill and a round of High Seat, Shivery Man and Blea Tarn

	1	2	3
grade			*
quality			
navigation			

ASSESSMENT: A classic, serious gill scramble: steep, damp and exciting. A rope is advised. Could be followed by a round of the quietest fells of the central lakes.

OS MAP: Outdoor Leisure 4
GR: 270197
DISTANCE: 16km (10 miles) via Ullscarf

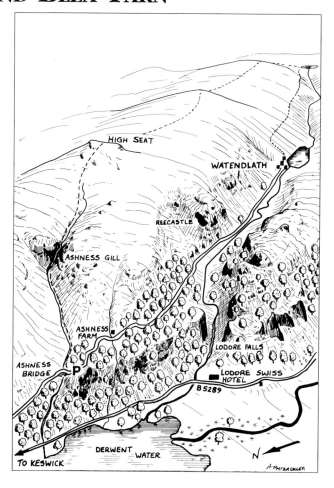

Within the bounds of Borrowdale there are several discoveries dating back to 1924, the year when Archer Thompson of Portinscale and his famous guide, Angelo Dibona wrote their names into the history of lakeland exploration.

It must have seemed strange to Dibona, whose native rocks were the high, dry and steep limestone cliffs of the Dolomites, to find himself seeking out moderate ways up the dank, vegetative crags and watercourses of Borrowdale. But in his case the piper was not calling the tune but simply hauling the rope. Of the routes they discovered in the summer of 1924, Ashness Gill must have seemed a most peculiarly English eccentricity. One wonders what Dibona made of it all or if the tale improved with the telling once he was back in some Dolomite refuge sharing a glass of heavy dark wine with fellow guides.

Thankfully for us Ashness Gill is not a major rock climb but an enjoyable, albeit damp, scramble up an interesting watercourse draining the fellside between Ashness Fell and Threefooted Brandreth on the north-west flank of High Seat. These are amongst the quietest and least frequented fells in the Lakes, even though they are above Borrowdale.

Today, routes like Ashness Gill receive little more than a mention in modern climbing guidebooks. From time to time, however, the gills find pride of place in winter climbing guides. Ashness Gill is a good example of that, as are Sandbed Gill in the Vale of St John and Taylor Gill on the way to Sty Head. All without exception provide superb ice climbs after a long, cold spell, often when there is little snow on the fells. A cold snap can produce ice pitches in the steeper gills to equal any on the higher crags. My introduction to Ashness a few winters ago was as it bristled in full icy armour. Armed with axes and crampons, we quickly frontpointed up the main fall during a day that involved a frantic round of Borrowdale in search of ephemeral ice. It is fair to say that it was easier in perfect winter conditions than in its normal summer state.

The route to Ashness Gill seems particularly pleasant. Taking the road signed to Watendlath, you cross the much photographed Ashness Bridge. Turn off the road into Strutta Wood. If it is your first visit, take time to walk up the slope behind the park and look out over Derwent Water. The road to Watendlath is very much on the tourist trail, being the heart of Walpole country and fictional home of Judith Paris, as those familiar with the Herries books will know.

Ashness Gill is close at hand (about 10 minutes walk away) and can be reached by following Barrow Beck, which cascades beneath Ashness Bridge, upstream. A very good path follows the true left bank of the stream and climbs alongside Ashness Gill which is a tributary of the beck falling in a steep, dark cascade. Obviously, it is best to wait until a dry spell has reduced the stream to a minimum,

although even then you must expect to get damp. This is a unique pleasure of gill scrambling and one about which I am sure sunburnt Dibona waxed lyrical, on his return to Italy! There's no record that Angelo Dibona ever repaid a visit to Ashness or any other Lakeland gill after the summer of 1924.

It is best to leave the path and join the main stream before Ashness Gill to become acquainted with the water and the nature of the rocks. Because of the trees and shady aspect of this watercourse, even after a drought (no rain for a weekend) the lichened rocks can be difficult. Vibrams may be altogether more comfortable for walking and dry rock but in wet or icy conditions they leave a lot to be desired. Dibona and Thompson, clad in their nailed mountain boots, would have had no problem whatsoever with lichened rocks. If you intend using a rope then you should also carry a selection of nuts as protection, as belays are not always obvious.

Where Ashness Gill joins the main stream you have to climb a rib that leads to a pool. The waterfall above this is reached by first traversing the right wall around another pool and then by climbing easier rocks on the left of the fall to reach a tree. Now it gets interesting and damp! Move back to the right, cross the stream and climb steeply past a dead tree to reach, with some difficulty, a damp ledge. You are now over a major hurdle, really the crux of the gill. Move back left above the falls and climb another cascade still on the left. Ledges above and to the right of this lead to a final waterfall

which can be climbed direct when frozen or dry but, when in between, it is best avoided by climbing steeply up the right wall, unless of course you like that sort of thing!

From the top of the gill it is simple enough to return down the path to Strutta Wood and go on to other scrambles in Borrowdale. However, to make an enjoyable round of it, join the path climbing to High Seat. If you found the gill dry you should take the opportunity to go on because the ground here is normally boggy. High Seat is the loftiest fell between Thirlmere and Derwent Water. The use of the word 'seat' is common in areas colonised by Norsemen and refers to a saeter, the high pastures used by animals in the fair summer months. Transhumance is typical in Alpine and Scandinavian countries and was naturally adopted on Lake District fells.

The rocks around the summit provide a welcome lookout from which to view the surrounding fells and must have served countless shepherds as such. Before Thirlmere was flooded for Manchester's use, these fells were the grazing grounds of Armboth Hall, now lost to the lake. Local rumour has it that a daughter of the Jacksons, who owned the Hall, married a noble white Russian to become Countess Ossalinsky. When Manchester bought Armboth Hall and the surrounding lands the Countess snubbed their first offer for her lands, holding out until, in the end, they paid her three times the original sum. Someone should have been made to pay far more for the right to

plant the miserable dark conifers that now blanket the fells around Thirlmere. Perhaps in the future when this crop is harvested the fells might be returned to more natural woodland or at least one that is in keeping with the district, without the straight lines.

Due south from High Seat the broad backed fells roll toward High Tove by way of The Pewits and Eddy Grave Stake. If you stay on the same course these almost featureless fells lead past strangely named Shivery Man to Blea Tarn beyond which romantically named Ullscarf ('notch of the wolf') beckons. Suprisingly, below the tops on the Thirlmere side these fells are quite complicated and interesting. With small hollows and rocky outcrops with knots of boggy ground and clear-flowing streams, this is the sheltered habitat of heron and deer.

The stream that flows from moraine-bound Blea Tarn flows into Watendlath Tarn and eventually into Derwent Water. The path follows the stream at first but then strikes out for Brimming Knott, Robinbank Crag and Rough Knott, skirting the fell above Watendlath to join the Thirlmere path above this tiny and beautifully situated hamlet. The way back to Ashness Bridge is not on the road but west of it, along a path on the far side of Watendlath Beck which passes below Caffel Side to recross the stream at a bridge near Moss Mire. This path then continues north through the wood to Ashness.

The final sparkling delights of Ashness Gill above the main fall

Route 3: NITTING HAWS, TIGGYWINKLE AND LITTLE TOWN

	1	2	3
grade			
quality			
navigation			

ASSESSMENT: A delightful scramble up an easily accessible ridge, providing an outstanding view over Borrowdale and an interesting route to the fell tops.

OS Map: Outdoor Leisure 4
GR: 250167
DISTANCE: 14km (9 miles) via Dale Head and Hindscarth

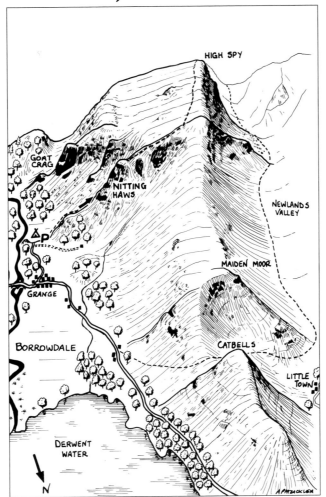

In 1772 William Gilpin wrote, 'This valley, so replete with hideous grandeur, is known by the name of the straits of Borrodale'. Today it seems a delightful playground with numerous outcrops providing endless diversion for climber and scrambler alike. More than any other, Shepherds Crag has become the tyro's mecca in recent years, with groups swarming over Brown Slabs and waiting in fearful anticipation at the foot of Little Chamonix. I have a son, William, who loves scrambling and exploring the low fells in equal measure but, like me, he enjoys them more when they mingle with the essential component, solitude. Despite its popularity and easy access you do not have to search far in Borrowdale for rough rock and solitude.

The campsite at Hollows Farm near Grange is a popular starting point for a day on the hill. With Beatrix Potter forming essential bedtime reading, many of our family outings have been in search of her characters. The thought of seeing Mrs Tiggywinkle on Cat Bells has been more motivating than a Mars Bar. As William has grown and become more adventurous his eyes are turned more and more to the steeper ridge lines and buttresses. Some of the easier scrambles have proved an ideal introduction to roped scrambling and rock climbing.

Close to Hollows Farm is Nitting Haws, jutting like a flying buttress from the hillside between Maiden Moor and High Spy. This delightful scramble follows the spur of Nitting Haws, also known as Knitting How, up a series of slabs and rocky steps separated by sections of walking, to a summit that provides an excellent balcony from which to view Derwent Water and Borrowdale. If you do not want to go on to the tops you can wander over to Jackdaw Ridge on Shepherds Crag or the Intake Ridge in Combe Gill.

Unlike many scrambles in Borrowdale this was not discovered by Bentley Beetham, of Everest fame, but by an even more famous duo, Archer Thompson and the guide Angelo Dibona in 1924. I can only assume they were in search of steeper ground or an alternative to the path as a way of climbing High Spy or they fancied a new route on the steep final buttress of Nitting Haws. The same pair also scrambled in Snowdonia where, on reaching the top of Crib Goch, Dibona suggested they turn back as a circuit of the Snowdon Horseshoe seemed out of the question without a bivouac.

From Grange it is a short walk to the camping field near Dalt Wood. A stile over the boundary wall leads from the field to the rough fell and almost immediately to the start of the scrambling which begins at the foot of the rock slabs above the corner of a walled plantation.

These easily angled slabs broken by vegetation lead to rock steps that land you at a terrace above which is a steeper band of rocks. A path leading left follows a grassy trod above a holly tree. Take this and gain a rock ramp marked by a second tree. Good holds let you squeeze past the tree up a small chimney onto the ramp above and so avoid the difficult,

steep rocks on the right. Follow the gantry for a few moves and then make a high step on the right on large holds to continue more easily up slabs to the top of this rocky step. This lands you on gently undulating ground with rocky outcrops rounded and polished by passing glaciers.

Walk and scramble over rock steps and grassy hollows to the foot of the next steepening in the ridge. Left of a ruined 'hut circle' is a spur of rock with a small juniper bush at its base. Above the juniper is a groove, slanting steeply right. Bridge up this on good holds and continue more easily over broken ground. This leads towards more difficult rock, partly hidden beneath dense juniper, which you avoid by traversing rightwards over rough scree to a more accommodating spur. Follow this through dark juniper and holly until you reach an obvious slab best passed on the left. The ground ahead is more broken and you must wind a way through trees, rocky steps and slabs, keeping more or less to the line of the ridge which ends at a small rock pinnacle below black overhangs which mark the final rock wall.

Avoid these overhangs by walking right beyond a large holly to a grassy bay where a groove allows you to scramble to the top of this step. Go up to another step, marked by a tree. Scramble behind the tree up a vegetative ramp leading diagonally right where an obvious break leads back left. There, good scrambling up a rocky crest leads to slab rock and the fine summit of Nitting Haws.

With half the climbing behind you it seems a shame not to go to the top by the path that climbs to the ridge between Maiden Moor and High Spy. A gentle day's walking would be to descend the ridge from Maiden Moor and go down by way of Hause Gate, then return southwards to Hollows Farm.

As part of a good day on the fells, Nitting Haws is a great way of starting a round of the high tops surrounding the Newlands Valley. Having gained the cairn on High Spy all is spread before you, but to see Newlands Beck you will have to climb out on the jutting prows above the deep-cut cliffs of Red Crag and Miners Crag. Dale Head's summit, above Great Gable and Dalehead Crags, looks close but to reach it you first have to descend to delightful Dalehead Tarn. If, like me, you linger too long by the reedy beck that falls from the tarn listening to the skylark you can always descend into Newlands. A good track leads northwards above the beck past ancient workings to Goldscope Mine. Developed by German mining engineers in the sixteenth century, its rich galena and copper deposits turned Newlands into one of the most important industrial centres in Britain.

If you can resist the ennui of the hills and manage the climb to Dale Head the tramp along Hindscarth Edge is guaranteed to keep you wide-eyed. Northwards, the impressive trench of Newlands frames distant Skiddaw. Hindscarth's rocky crest falls in a long spur from High Crags descending steeply to Low Snab

where a footbridge crosses the river to Goldscope Mine, corrupted from the German *Gottes Gabt,* God's gift. Continue on the path northwards to Little Town, where those familiar with Mrs Tiggywinkle will be reminded of Lucy and will take in their stride the steady pull up the west flank of Cat Bells to Hause Gate. With Derwent Water spread before you, descend on the diagonal path to Manesty and continue to Grange.

An alternative to dropping into Newlands and a very different walk altogether is to traverse from Dale Head to shallow Launchy Tarn with its fine views of Gillercombe and Green Gable to the south. From the white rock and dark heather surrounding the tarn, descend south-east over open fell to pick up a path that follows the outtake wall above Seatoller that leads north to Tongue Gill. Here the path joins the Cumbria Way (Allerdale Ramble) and continues to Castle Crag through National Trust woodland to the lovely stone-bedded River Derwent and Grange.

Sallie O'Connor scrambling up the lower rib of Nitting Haws. Grange can be seen below and Skiddaw is in the distance

Route 4: THE GABLES VIA SOURMILK GILL AND RABBIT'S TROD

	1	2	3
grade (Sourmilk Gill)	*		
grade (Rabbit's Trod)			
quality			
navigation			

ASSESSMENT: Two contrasting scrambles combined with a strenuous walk over high fells amongst some of the grandest rock scenery the Lake District has to offer.

GR: 235121
OS MAP: Outdoor Leisure 4
DISTANCE: 10km (6.5 miles) with a lot of ascent and descent

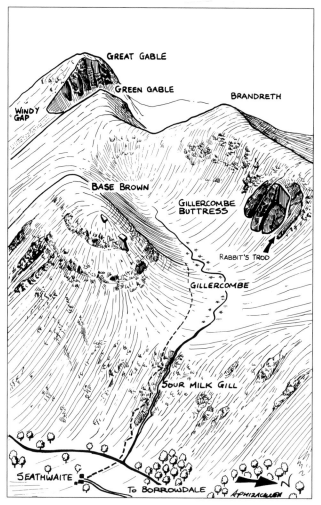

'A man may love climbing and care nought for mountain scenery; he may love scenery and hate climbing; or he may equally be devoted to both. Those who are most attracted to mountains are those who, to the fullest extent, possess both these sources of enjoyment – those who can combine fun and frolic of a splendid sport with the indefinable delight of lovely form, tone and colouring.'

The words of A. F. Mummery just about sum up the delights of scrambling which for me is the purest mountain pursuit. The finest scrambles are exhilarating challenges that demand skill, concentration and free-flowing movement without the need of a rope for the most part. But as scramblers we are twice blessed: our playground is amongst the most profound scenery the hills have to offer – the airy ridges, steep buttresses and thundering fern-filled gills.

There are times when its is difficult to define where scrambling ends and rock climbing begins. It could be argued that climbing begins when safe movement depends on the rope, the need to belay and the necessity of climbing one at a time. But difficulty and danger, like beauty, are in the eye of the beholder.

Take, for example, Gillercomb Buttress above Seathwaite at the head of Borrowdale. Like much of the valley it was neglected by climbers until the early part of this century. Bentley Beetham, an Everest pioneer and the champion

of Borrowdale scrambling and climbing, recalled in the 1953 Fell and Rock guidebook to the area that 'in the eighteenth century a long, strong rope was kept in Borrowdale, by subscription, for the purpose of letting men down into the rocks to take the nest and young eagles'. Today there are no eagles left on Gillercomb. But if the eagles have long shunned the place, there are, thanks to Beetham's exploration, rocks where rabbits can dare! From a casual glance Gillercomb may not appear scrambling terrain, and therein lies the joy of the sport and the reward for having an eye for a line and route-finding skill.

The farm at Seathwaite is the starting point of many a lakeland jaunt. Paths lead off towards Glamara, Great End, Scafell and the Gables, both Green and Great. One of the most enjoyable days I know combines two equally worthwhile scrambles. The first up Sourmilk Gill is a worthy contender in its own right, providing over 300m of good scrambling, whilst the second, Rabbit's Trod, is exceptional but on the limit of scrambling terrain where rope and belaying techniques are essential to safety. To combine these with a round of Green Gable and Great Gable, and the option of descending Westmorland Crag to Sphinx Rock and returning to Seathwaite via Styhead Tarn, is to experience a great lakeland day on the mountains.

Ronnie Faux well poised on Sourmilk Gill

There has long been a general rule amongst hill walkers that you should always avoid following unknown mountain streams when descending in bad weather. They are dangerous because the rocks are invariably slippery and drop over unseen falls. However, for the scrambler looking to gain high ground these are the very places that can offer the most enjoyable route – which in the point of this tale!

SOURMILK GILL

The path to Gillercomb from Seathwaite goes under the arch in a barn opposite the farm, crosses the bridge and climbs steeply left of Sourmilk Gill, but here scramblers leave the path for the stream bed. The route up the gill rises as the river falls, in a series of steps. The route hugs a rocky line between water and fellside. The rock is sound, rough and dappled by water – except after a dry spell when water-worn slabs, egg-shell smooth, are revealed, glistening and naked. Begin by boulder hopping and scrambling easily up its true left bank until the first large fall is reached, with a deep plungepool at its base. The slabs on the right provide good sport, with the surest and driest climbing away from the stream. However, the difficulties on this side of the gill soon ease.

If you are looking for sport, cross the stream to a rowan tree, red-berried in early autumn and climb the rocks on the left. Ahead, the best scrambling is to be found on the left of the gill. In spate, the stream really lives up to its name by providing a cascade of creamy water. The rough rock offers plenty of options, although the best climbing is once again on the other bank. Keep following the stream to another small fall, which can be avoided on the left, and continue up the central rib which leads to an amphitheatre. The feel of the spray as you scramble from hold to ledge adds a new dimension to the game and the thundering fury of the falls produces a powerful atmosphere – the scrambler's equivalent of an Alpine grand course. The stream ahead flows down a clean-cut channel, with the rib on the left providing the best scrambling. The rock is good and leads to a Rowan tree where an obvious ramp runs close to the fall before ending in the marshy hollow of Gillercomb.

Gill scrambling is a magical game of 'greased poles' and infinite beauty, something that Mummery experienced and Ruskin, I fear, did not. The climber is privy to the mountain's secrets: lichen-dappled slabs, cracks, crevices and whirlpool hollows, water-worn over aeons to become botanical gems of ferns, mosses and arctic alpines. Hidden from general view, they become the preserve of those who are willing to climb the 'greasy pole'.

On the hillside to the right as you scrambled up you can pick out the spoilheaps of mines that once produced their own version of 'black gold': plumbago or 'wadd' as it is known locally. This was pure graphite which, in the sixteenth

A flying glimpse of Gillercomb showing Sourmilk Gill, Raven Crag and an unusual view of Pillar and Ennerdale

century, was highly prized for shot and mould-making, for use in medicine and, of course, for fine-pointed lakeland pencils. The mines were guarded day and night, and by an Act of Parliament, but still an industry developed amongst locals for smuggling wadd across the fells. Perhaps the best known of these was Moses Rigg who was also famous for brandy smuggling: it was landed on the coast near St Bee's and transported along a path known now as Moses Trod which drops into Wasdale.

RABBIT'S TROD

To reach Rabbit's Trod cross the floor of the cwm and aim for the lowest rocks of Raven Crag below Grey Knotts. A dry stone wall leads almost to the start of the route. Beetham's Fell and Rock Climbing Club guidebook to Borrowdale points out the fine sport to be had on the upper Seathwaite Slabs to the right of Sourmilk Gill before you reach Raven Crag. They provide an enjoyable diversion *en route* to higher things. Rabbit's Trod, graded 'moderately difficult' in Beetham's guide, can with a little variation provide 250m of scrambling which means avoiding the original crux chimney near the top by following easier ground to the right. This route provides exposed scrambling up easy, angled slabs, involving thoughtful and continuous work. The slabs are on the right of the crag bounding the right-hand side of an obvious scree-filled gully which falls from a grassy rake. The scrambling begins at the foot of these slabs and is marked by a small cairn.

Climb the open slabs by following the easiest line which sweeps leftwards to a rib bounding the scree-filled gully. Fine scrambling leads to a heathery brake, rending right at first and then back left towards the gully. Continue up the open slabs on good rock to reach a small col, about 125m from the start, which is overlooked by the steep wall of the main crag.

The rock ahead is steeper, with the best scrambling nearer the gully. Follow the easiest line until you can reach ledges that lead to the obvious grassy terrace. It is worth taking the time to look from this eagle's perch towards the distant skyline of Helvellyn, Skiddaw and Blencathra and let your mind follow the liquid silver streams that etch the lakeland landscape. Continue more or less up a ridge, climbing a steeper wall to below two chimney cracks. These are the crux of Rabbit's Trod but are best turned on the right by an easier corner. All that remains is to follow the easiest rocks up an edge to the top. This is a superb position high above the main crag.

At the top of the crag a faint path leads to the top of Grey Knotts. Alternatively, you can traverse the fellside towards 'three footed' Brandreth. Between Grey Knotts and Gillercomb Head the route follows a broad-backed ridge, picking its way amongst a series of stunning tarns that on a still day reflect the mountain giants that surround them. The largest of them, though not large at all by lakeland standards, is Grey Knotts Tarn, followed by

Brandreth's Three Tarns. Following markers on the main path that skirts Gillercomb Head, it is easy to arrive at Green Gable whose summit provides a fine vantage point. Looking north-west the long corridor of dark forested Ennerdale draws the eye whilst, in the opposite direction, the Pikes and the distant, unmistakeable form of Ingleborough can be seen on a clear day. Much closer, across the slash of the Windy Gap that separates the Gables, is the magnificent rock architecture of Gable Crag, host to a multitude of stunning rock climbs. The route descends steeply into the gap and scrambles up rock steps on the right of the main path on the edge of the crag, to find a scramblers variation at the top.

From the summit of the Gable the sporting route back to Seathwaite is to descend south-west to the large and obvious Westmorland Cairn. Set above the precipitous crags, it provides a spectacular panorama of Wastwater and Scafell. Below, you can pick out a track leading to the top of Napes Crag before descending steeply alongside rocky Sphinx Ridge. Gain the track, best reached by skirting Westmorland Crag to the west, and descend the steep, scrambly path until you are level with the inscrutable face of Sphinx Rock. Here, a path known as the Climbers Traverse skirts below Napes Needle, Hell's Gate and the fine, much-photographed walls of Kern Knotts to the rescue box at Sty Head where a huge path follows the gill north-east, by way of Taylorgill Force, back to Seathwaite.

Route 5: COMBE GILL: INTAKE RIDGE AND DOVENEST CRAG

	1	2	3
grade (Intake Ridgel)			
grade (Attic Cave)		*	
quality			
navigation			

ASSESSMENT A combination of two very contrasting scrambles hidden in one of the most delightful valleys in the district, steeped in history.

OS MAP: Outdoor Leisure 4
GR: 249136
DISTANCE: 8km (5 miles)

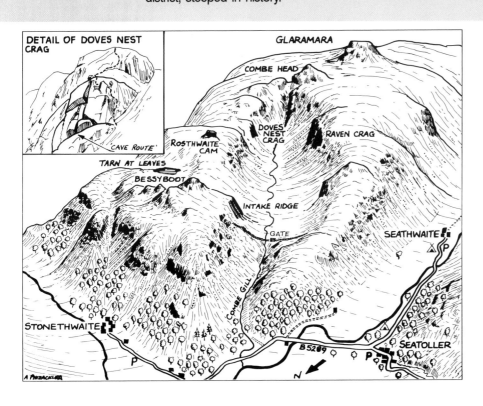

I think it was Alf Wainwright, God bless him, who said he preferred maps to books, a sentiment I share most of the time. Despite my love of maps I am dismayed how often my plans seem to fall across two of them or, worse still, along the weathered, unintelligible fold of a single sheet.

If you too have a penchant for maps then the broad and complicated head of Borrowdale certainly merits scrutiny. At Rosthwaite, where the meandering Derwent has left a broad meadow, a fistful of becks tumble from U-shaped valleys spreading like fingers of an open hand. To begin, the Derwent flows from Seathwaite where it collects Sourmilk, Taylor and Grains gills; fine scrambles all. Hause Gill, another important tributary, thunders from the slaty heights of Honister, whilst quiet Stonethwaite Beck tumbles from Langstrath, nurtured by Angle Tarn between Esk Hause, Bowfell and Rossett Pike. Yet of all Borrowdale's delights, the valley that spawns Combe Gill, nestling between Rosthwaite and Seatoller, offers the most unusual scrambling.

The Combe remains a peaceful place when Seathwaite is seething and Borrowdale is blocked by summer visitors. This hanging valley is far from obvious, cloaked as it is by hills sweeping from Thornythwaite Fell over Raven Crags towards Glaramara and Combe Head and on its eastern side by Rosthwaite Fell and strangely named Bessyboot. It has long been a favourite of mine for summer evening soloing, the glaciated slab on the Intake Crag

providing an alternative to that beside Sourmilk Gill. Only minutes from the parking along the road to Thorneythwaite Farm, the gill holds deep, cool pools ideal for skinny dipping at the end of a hot day.

As with much of Borrowdale's climbing, it was Bentley Beetham who was responsible for exploring its scattered crags and bringing them to the attention of climbers. A decade or so before his onslaught, that great lakeland eccentric, Millican Dalton, self-styled 'professor of adventure', discovered the dark confines of the Dove Nest Cave.

A free spirit, Millican Dalton gave up normal work in 1905 to live amongst mountains and earn his living as a guide. During the warm summer months his home was a cave in Borrowdale, close to Castle Crag, from where he supplemented his diet with nuts and berries gathered on the fells. A figure after Crusoe, he wore homemade clothes, a feather in his cap and sailed a rickety raft across Derwent Water. He was still climbing at the age of eighty and died during the long, cruel winter of 1947. His attitude to life, summed up by Dr Mabel Baker in *Cumbrian Rock*, seems less eccentric and most sensible to me.

He did things on the rocks, as everywhere else, to please himself, but not for self seeking; to fit in with his theory on life, and

Tim Naylor at the start of the Intake Ridge

of earth and his relation to it. He believed that people (astronomers included) were shutting their eyes to the foundation of the universe. Perhaps he was wiser than most of us and his long happy life trod a pathway to the stars.

There is a lot for the scrambler in Combe Gill. This is a marvellous combination of scrambles which combine with a walk to Combe Head and on to Glaramara before a violent thirst inevitably pulls me to the Langstrath for a pint.

Intake Ridge

This scramble begins with the Intake Ridge, discovered by Beetham in 1937. You follow the track into Combe Gill through a coppice of holly and rowan, red-berried in autumn, to a gate in the Intake Wall. Finding the scramble is simplicity itself. Follow the wall leftwards across the stream and up the fellside to the base of the ridge which is the start of the route. Ahead lies over 185m of scrambling, broken in places, easy to avoid but with the main sections interesting and exposed. In the original *Fell and Rock Climbing Club guide to Borrowdale* by Bentley Beetham the Intake was described in twelve separate pitches and graded 'moderate'. You can always find good belays should you use a rope and it can be well protected.

Starting at the lowest rocks of the ridge where they meet the wall, climb the first short step and then descend right to the continuation of the ridge. Climb a steep wall on the left and then some knobbly slabs before following a gangway leftwards, below a group of trees, where you reach easier ground.

The route past broken rocks leads to a corner where a slab trends rightwards to an exposed position on the edge of polished slabs. The next moves are the crux and you have a choice: either follow a crack slanting diagonally rightwards, or cross the lower slab on the right followed by easier, exposed scrambling to the top. These slabs offer a variety of interesting rock problems and are ideal for introducing novices to climbing. This is how Beetham came to discover them in the first place.

Continue up the rock spur on the left to a buttress which is climbed to the right of a rocky bulge. Large holds lead up a heathery wall followed by scrambling over broken ground. Move right and follow easy ground to the top where you can discover the beautifully named Tarn at Leaves. From the top of the scramble it is possible to descend a faint sheep trod and contour rough ground to the foot of Dovenest Crag. This was once a popular playground for climbers, but the forces of nature are still at work and the block that long ago slipped to form the caves is still affected by gravity! The original troglodytes' excursion, through the Rat Hole, was once highly recommended but has been rendered dangerous by the slip. As Archer Thompson wrote in 1925, 'The place is quite unlike anything else in the whole of the Lake district.... it is a rare natural phenomena [sic]'.

Attic Cave

Avoid the subterranean pleasures described by Beetham and opt instead for the safe alternative of the 'Attic Cave', originally pitch eight of the Rat Hole climb. It begins with a traverse from the right along a platform leading to a deep cleft in the face of the crag. Enter the confines of the cleft and climb a narrow chimney. Instead of entering the black Rat Hole on the right, follow a terrace leftwards into the open where a step gives entry into a V-groove. Easy jamming followed by an exposed move takes you right to a platform. Overhung and undercut, a strenuous pull on huge holds deposits you on the balcony of the Attic Cave where I am always reminded of Beetham's 1953 guide: 'One often hears that the Doves' Nest is the place to go in wet weather, and although it is true that by doing so you get out of the rain, it does not follow that you get out of the wet, for water may be found dripping from the roof and streaming down the walls and onto unskilfully shielded candles.'

At this point you begin to wonder about getting back. Do not despair; simply reverse the route of ascent – much easier than it looks! There is plenty more scrambling to be had in the valley. Combe Gill itself forms a deep-cut gully at the head of the valley. It provides a fierce, wet scramble with some difficult cave pitches and should only be contemplated after a long, dry spell.

Route 6: CAM CRAG RIDGE, LANGSTRATH

	1	2	3
grade		*	
quality			
navigation			

ASSESSMENT: A fine approach walk followed by a long, open scramble up clean, solid rock with good views of the central fells.

OS MAP: Outdoor Leisure 4
GR: 268133, Stonethwaite campsite
DISTANCE: 8km (5 miles) via Tarn at Leaves; 12km (7.5 miles) via Glaramara

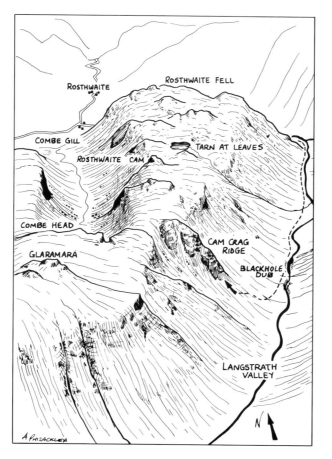

ROSTHWAITE
ROSTHWAITE FELL
COMBE GILL
TARN AT LEAVES
ROSTHWAITE CAM
COMBE HEAD
GLARAMARA
CAM CRAG RIDGE
BLACKHOLE DUB
LANGSTRATH VALLEY
N
A. PHIZACKLEA

This is one of Bentley Beetham's countless 'three star' discoveries, first climbed in 1943 with J.B. Meldrum and members of the Goldsborough Club. In my opinion it should be saved for a time when the fells have been blessed by hot weather and the rocks have absorbed the summer's heat and are as warm as fire stones. Not that this scramble needs a long spell of good weather to dry out; in fact it can be done in almost any conditions throughout the year. But if you really want to enjoy yourself wait for Langstrath Beck to drop and the rocks to warm. Without doubt, this stream has some of the best bathing pools in the Lakes, comparable with the upper Esk.

You can find parking at the campsite beyond the pub at Stonethwaite. Follow the path southeast by Greenup Gill as far as the confluence with Langstrath Beck which becomes a roaring hole in spate. The stony track soon emerges from the shade of trees into the flat-floored Langstrath. Follow the track, part of the Cumbria Way, for a couple of kilometres of easy open walking until the long arm of Cam Crag Ridge is easily identified on the right. By now, if you have taken my advice, you will be hot and ready for a dip. At a point where a fence crosses the path the stream has cut a deep gorge perhaps 30m long. This is Blackmoss Pot, used in the past as a sheep dub but in reality made for skinny dipping! For the enthusiastic sampler of such streams there are two approaches: either strip off and dive in at the top where the water is deep and there are flat diving platforms and swim down the length of its mini-gorge; or for those seeking delayed gratification a sporting, if tentative, approach is by way of a traverse of the steep sidewalls. Both will ensure a refreshing dip in the dub.

Having cooled off, get on with the business of scrambling. A trod leads diagonally up to the bottom of the ridge where the huge Woof Stones guard access to the start. These provide plenty of good bouldering before the ascent of the ridge, the start of which is obvious. A track leads to a bouldery start and the foot of the lowest rocks of the ridge, narrow at first but finally merging into the broad rounded rock buttress that is Cam Crag Ridge. Ascend sound rock on good holds to the top of the first rise to land at a grassy bay. Beyond lies a buttress with the best scrambling up its edge by way of a series of cracks and corners. There is a choice of lines all invariably on good rock laced with quartzy veins. Simply follow your nose, continuing up slabs of firm rough rock to the top.

Once at the top, there are a number of choices on offer. You can descend for another dip in the dub or cross the ridge and descend steeply into Combe Gill for more scrambling on Dovenest Crag (see page 35). This is a delightful hanging valley with lots of scrambling and middle-grade rock climbing. In winter it even sports one of the most popular gully

The author finishing a steep section of Cam Crag Ridge

climbs in the district. Alternatively, if you want a summit and a longer walk follow the vague ridge top around Combe Head and climb to the summit of Glaramara. A strange name, Glaramara is a compound of several words and means, 'a mountain with a shieling by the ravines'. In 1210, apparently, it was spelt Hovedgleuermerhe!

For a quick return, head north to Thornythwaite Fell from the head of Combe Gill and descend to the Combe. Cross to the true right bank of the stream and descend a well-marked path to the mouth of the Combe where you can pick up a trod leading to Stonethwaite. Here you might just be lucky and find the pub open.

A bird's eye view of Cam Crag Ridge

Route 7: HEAD OF NEWLANDS: LOWTHWAITE CRAG AND DALE HEAD PILLAR

grade (Lowthwaite Crag)	1	2	3
	*		
grade (Dale Head Pillar)			
quality			
navigation			

ASSESSMENT: A delightful round of the Newlands skyline that connects some easy and enjoyable scrambling, with the finest views in the north-western fells.

Quality note: * but a *** walk
OS MAP: Outdoor Leisure 4
GR: 234196
DISTANCE: 12km (7.5 miles) via Hindscarth and Scope End 13km (8 miles) via Robinson and Little Dale

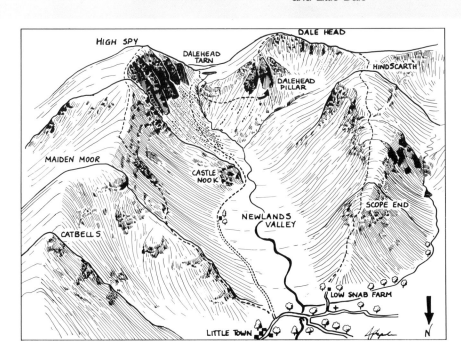

From a scrambling point of view the north-western fells are quite disappointing. You would have thought that the forces that formed Grisedale Pike, Hopgill Head, Crag Hill and Sail would have exposed more climbable rock. The map seems to suggest that there is plenty to have a go at, but having gone at it with a vengeance there is surprisingly little to report that is of continuous interest. In winter conditions the rocks of Hopcarton Crag offered some sport but in summer they are much too loose to be recommended. Even quiet Newlands can provide little in the way of long or continuous rock or gill scrambling. However, what there is is enjoyable and, in any case, the situation makes up for the lack of lines and difficulty. Castle Nook was disappointing, so perhaps Newlands can remain a valley where we can pioneer our own lines to the fell tops.

One of the most enjoyable scrambles, and certainly one of the most logical, can be found at the very end of the Newlands Valley on Dale Head Pillar. Unfortunately, it is a long valley and a direct ascent to the Pillar seems less than logical. What is far more attractive is a high-level round of the fells surrounding Newlands that takes in as much scrambling as possible.

From Little Town, of Lucy fame for those familiar with Beatrix Potter's stories, you can follow the level miners' track towards Goldscope mine. It takes a vivid imagination to think of this valley as an industrial centre of

great importance but that is what it was. For more than 2,000 years these mountains have been mined. Newlands was rich in copper and lead and also had a rich silver deposit, although the latter soon ran out. Of gold there was only a trace; enough to excite prospectors and mining engineers since Roman times but not enough to bring prosperity. Of those engineers who explored the valley's wealth, the most important was Daniel Hechstetter from Augsburg in Germany. He went on to found the Company of Mines Royal in the reign of Elizabeth I. The year was 1561 and this was the first mining company to be formed in the North of England. Ore from the Newlands Valley and elsewhere in Cumbria was transported to Copperheap Bay on the shores of Derwent Water for processing. Names like Copperheap record its past industry and a time when its smeltworks was the most important in Britain. The track that leads into Newlands from Little Town was constructed to connect the mines of the valley with the processing works at Copperheap Bay and Silver Hill before going to the smeltworks of Keswick on the banks of the Greta. John Postlethwaite, in his book *Mines and Mining In The Lake District* (1889), writes that 'the smelting works then erected at Keswick were the largest in England, and probably in Europe, at that time.' He records that, by 1565, there were seven smelt mills

Newlands Valley from Dale Head, once the industrial hub of Cumbria

around Keswick including Dale Head, Stoney Croft Gill, Braithwaite, Thornthwaite, Roughtengill and Greenside. There were also two iron furnaces at Langdale and Langstrath. Today it is hard to imagine a scene filled with people, industry and spewing smoke from the furnaces in full blast when you look down on the town from Maiden Moor or Cat Bells.

LOWTHWAITE CRAG

From almost opposite Low Snab it is possible to piece together an interesting albeit disconnected route east up the broken fellside above Lowthwaite Crag. The rock is good but is fairly covered in vegetation. When I scrambled here, peregrines were nesting on Lowthwaite Crag and buzzards circled above me. Near the top I crossed Barnes Gill and found a way on to Maiden Moor by way of Bull Crag. It was an enjoyable scramble simply because I was finding my own way and was quite alone. It was possible to leave it at any point but I did find one or two real boulder problems. Above all, it was a perfect summer's evening and by the time I had walked along Narrow Moor to High Spy the sun was already low over Sail and Crag Hill and the bracken on Hindscarth glowed like burnished gold.

On a clear day the walk around the Newlands skyline offers extensive views. It seems as if High Spy and Dale Head are centre stones from which to look out across the whole of the district. What you actually realise is how incredibly compact a mountain range this is

compared with those of Scotland or even Wales. The old school geography books describe the Lake District as similar to a wheel, with the Gables like a hub at its centre and the major valleys radiating from it like spokes.

By the time you get to High Spy the deeply incut rocks of Red Crag and Miners Crag look as though they should hold more than a few rock climbs. Unfortunately, they are not good and thus few make the effort to reach them. Across the head of the valley opposite, it is possible to spy the line of Dale Head Pillar which starts on the lowest rocks of Gable Crag.

DALE HEAD PILLAR

To reach the start you must first get to the stream issuing from lovely Dalehead Tarn. The path descends into the narrows alongside Newlands Beck and should be left here to reach the lowest rocks of the broad buttress of Great Gable below Dale Head. Although there is plenty of rock hereabouts it is north- facing, broken, heavily covered in vegetation and subsequently slow to dry – apart from that, it is perfect for our needs!

To the right of the base of the buttress a grassy ramp slants leftwards. Take this for about a rope's length before moving right along a grassy terrace as far as a rowan tree. Behind it climb upwards until it is possible to move right once again across slabby rock which quickly leads to easier ground. The rock above now deteriorates, so stay with the easier footing on the right until the crag above steepens and an

obvious route slants back leftwards across the narrowing buttress. Follow this to the edge where you can overlook the gully that defines the left side of the buttress. The scrambling above is quite straightforward and in a good position, exposed to the gully. All too soon the scrambling runs out and a path continues to the summit of Dale Head.

One of the most impressive things about Dale Head is the view from its summit down broad Newlands. It is a glorious sight, made even more so by the bulk of Skiddaw rising above flat meadows filling the space between Bassenthwaite and Derwent Water. Having enjoyed the views of Borrowdale from Maiden Moor and High Spy and those of Ennerdale from Dale Head, the vista now changes to one of Buttermere and Crummock Water, Fleetwith Pike, High Stile, Red Pike and distant Pillar.

It is tempting to go on north-west to Robinson, even though it involves quite a pull. If you do, then the natural return leg would be into Little Dale and Scope Beck and the narrow lane that runs to Little Town by way of the church.

The logical skyline route takes the path that curves around Hindscarth Crags dipping slightly to a hause before the gentle rise to the summit of Hindscarth (Old Norse for 'pass of the red deer'). There should be no navigational problems from here to the farm at Low Snab. The narrowing ridge extends over High Crags to Scope End where a path crosses to Goldscope and you meet the miners' track returning to Little Town.

Dale Head and its crags from High Spy

Route 8: HONISTER CRAG AND THE DELIGHTS OF HAY STACKS AND HIGH STILE

	1	2	3
grade			*
quality			
navigation			

ASSESSMENT: A serious and steep scramble through impressive and, at times, loose terrain that can nevertheless be well protected with a rope; followed by a long, high-level ridge walk on the south side of Buttermere.

OS MAP: Outdoor Leisure 4
GR: 195150, Gatescarth Farm or 218143, a lay-by
DISTANCE: 22km (14 miles) via Floutern Tarn 16.5km (10 miles) via Red Pike and Scale Beck

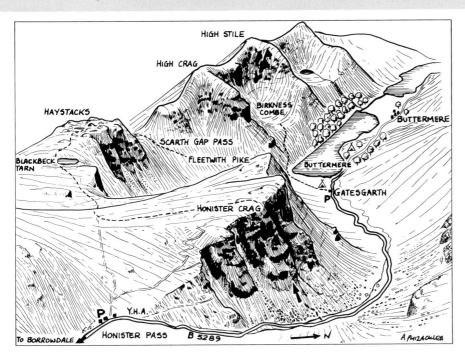

Honister can seem a dark and awesome place. The approach from either side is steep and unrelenting. From Seatoller the road climbs steeply alongside Hause Gill into Little Gatesgarthdale to where the valley widens and the beck meanders before Honister Hause and the youth hostel. Here at the very hause the fells are shattered and scattered with monuments to human toil. I almost expect to see these words from Ozymandias, 'Look upon my works, ye Mighty, and despair'.

I well remember the first time I crossed the pass and the deep impression it left. We had hiked from a camp near Castle Rock in St John's in the Vale and crossed Greenup Edge in thick mist and gentle rain by the path from Wythburn. By the time we descended Greenup Gill to Stonethwaite the thought of hauling our soaked bodies and heavy packframes to the pass held little appeal. Alas we had agreed a rendezvous with friends at Dub's Hut in the slate workings on Fleetwith Pike and had no intention of missing it. It had been converted from a ruined slate works building into a climbing hut by Keswick Mountaineering Club and was said to be haunted. We were late reaching the top of the pass, foot sore from lugging our loads into the force of a wet westerly howling over its brow. The road ahead seemed to drop into a black hole that was Buttermere, whilst our track, the quarry level, climbed relentlessly into the

gathering gloom and imagined danger. We eventually found the hut and climbed into its multi-storey bunks exhausted. It was a sleep that not even a ghostly quarryman, Lanty Slee or Moses Rigg himself could have disturbed. That was more than 30 years ago but even today crossing the Honister Hause can leave me with a strong impression.

It is not only the pass that is memorable. This scramble crosses some equally impressive ground and has a forbidding atmosphere. The slatey walls hereabouts are steep with ledges covered in loose talus from the old workings on a face where grass and scree seem to defy Nature's laws of equilibrium. Having said all that, a scramble up steep Honister Crag provides a real adventure that can, if needs must, be well protected using a rope and sound belaying techniques. However, it is a serious proposition, being long, exposed and in places difficult, and is best done when the rocks have dried and the lichen is no longer a menace.

From whatever side of the pass you approach, park in a lay-by between the Maiden Stone and the small road bridge on the Buttermere side of the pass. Above you the north-facing flank of Fleetwith Pike is dark, dank and awesome, just the place for a scramble! The joy of this route is that it finds a way through improbable terrain to provide an exciting line to the fell tops.

Open scrambling up easy angled slabs and ribs on the lower section of Honister Crag

From the lay-by the jutting rocks of broad Honister Crag are obvious. The crag is split into two buttresses by a deep gully well marked on the map. The eastern buttress, contained between Wet Knotts and Black Star on the map, is the one to aim for. It is possible, though not very pleasant, to climb steeply up scree to the foot of the buttress. The scramble starts well left of the big gully up a series of easy, angled slabs covered with an unfair mixture of grass and loose stones. These give way to scree which in turn can be crossed to the foot of a steeper wall of secure rock, thankfully. Climb this on good holds and gain another scree shoot. Steep rock over on the right can be climbed and leads in turn to another buttress which is broken and has vegetation. The easiest way up this follows grassy terraces grazed by sheep which cross a vegetative gully cutting through some steep ground. Climb this hollow which looks like a black hole from below.

Taking care with the rock, climb leftwards along a ramp towards a cannon-like, perched rock. This is exposed and quite serious but can be well protected by use of a rope. Once at the block enjoy the view of the pass, as you have undoubtedly earned it. The way ahead still remains exposed. Move left along a ledge that ends in a slab. Right of the slab, steep climbing up heathery steps leads to a well defined rib. Make a difficult move left to reach better things. A flake provides an airy traverse left, every bit as impressive as my first view of the pass and certainly a lot more serious. This

exposed work leads to a much more amenable rake and the end of the major difficulties, but not the scramble.

From here another terrace slants across the crag face to a tree. Easy ground left of the tree lands you on a quarry incline which can be followed past precarious mine workings to the top of the crag.

With the serious business behind you, the rest of the round is pure enjoyment. Having reached the top of Fleetwith Pike the whole panorama of peaks that form the skyline ridge surrounding Warnscale Beck opens out: first Grey Knotts, then Brandreth, Hay Stacks, High Crag, High Stile and Red Pike. For good measure and completeness you should consider taking in Starling Dodd and Great Borne. Of course it is possible to leave the ridge for Buttermere at any number of natural breaks; for instance, directly down Fleetwith Edge, at Scarth Gap or Red Pike. The complete traverse of the southern heights of Buttermere is a wonderful hike and the return from boggy Floutern Tarn to Scales Beck and the banks of Crummock and Buttermere is a delight.

The first leg is simple enough. Follow the old levels down to the old Drum House on the tramway path that cuts from Honister to Dub's Quarry and gain the summit of Grey Knotts. Easier walking then leads via a plethora of pools to the cairn of Brandreth. For those wanting another scramble it's possible to contour around Grey Knotts to the foot of Raven Crag and scramble up Rabbit's Trod (p.30).

Brandreth provides the first clear views into long Ennerdale and the ridge ahead which forms the high watershed between it and Buttermere. The next leg is enjoyable rambling north-west towards the mirror-like pool of Blackbeck Tarn. The path makes a dog-leg turn around Loft Beck and climbs to lovely Innominate Tarn. There are plenty of unnamed tarns on these fells but this one is actually named, nameless or innominate, by the Ordnance Survey and it seems it will remain so. It was a favourite spot of Alf Wainwright (AW) whose ashes were spread close by. A lot of AW fans wanted to rename Innominate Tarn as Wainwright Tarn but sensibly his widow resisted the gesture. Strangely enough, this was once called Loaf Tarn, a prosaic name that seems to have been dropped. Whatever its real name is, the views from around its rocky hollow are stunning.

From Hay Stacks the path drops steeply to Scarth Gap, linking Buttermere and Ennerdale. The next leg is the least pleasant of the round, in many ways, but it soon ends. The ridge rises first over the hummock of Seat and then by way of the scree-covered slope of Gamlin End to the summit of High Crag. It is a bit of a sweat toiling up this loose path but at least there are good views of Pillar to the south and, once at the top, the walk around the head of Birkness Comb above precipitous Eagle Crag is a delightful contrast.

The views from the top of High Crag are as good as can be found anywhere in the Lakes. Below are the lakes of Ennerdale, Crummock and Buttermere and all around are the highest peaks in Cumbria. In the distance can be spotted a silver seam of the sea to the west. Late in the day it provides some of the finest sunsets in the district. But ramble on to Red Pike around the head of Chapel Crags and you will see why the Pike is so called. The eroded path down The Saddle towards Bleaberry Tarn cuts an ugly scar into the blood-coloured earth of the fellside.

If, at this stage, the sun has already set then it is best to descend to Bleaberry Tarn and return by way of Birkness Wood to Gatescarth Farm and the road. If there is daylight left and your legs are willing, skirt round Lingcombe Edge and descend westwards, via Little Dodd to Starling Dodd and on to the shelter cairn on Great Borne, once a popular viewpoint. From here, descend northwards to Floutern Tarn, where the boggy ground will certainly cool off your feet, and , for a while at least, the route is all downhill. Scale Beck leads quickly to Crummock Water where it is not far across meadows to the village of Buttermere. Suitably refreshed, it is not far along the lakeside back to the lay-by below Honister Crag. Of course, if you saw the sunset from High Stile you may be too late for last orders.

Scrambling near Hay Stacks above Buttermere

Route 9: GREY CRAG BY WAY OF HARROW BUTTRESS AND CHOCKSTONE RIDGE, BIRKNESS COMB

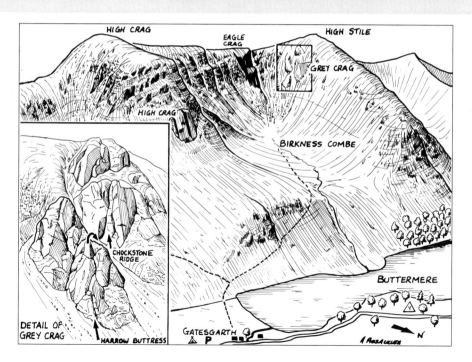

	1	2	3
grade			*
quality			
navigation			

ASSESSMENT: Continuous, exposed scramble combining two routes up a fine, firm buttress, marking the technical limit of scrambling. Good belays and ledges.

OS MAP: Outdoor Leisure 4
GR: 195150, Gatesgarth Farm
DISTANCE: 7km (4.5 miles) via Scarth Gap; 10.5km (6.5 miles) via Fleetwith Pike

The question is often asked, 'When does a scramble become a rock climb?' Undoubtedly there is a fine line between the two; a line that is often crossed, perhaps only for a move or two, but it is enough to quicken the pulse and set alarm bells ringing. Scrambling is a serious game, perhaps the most potentially dangerous one played in the mountains. The scrambler who enjoys going unroped needs judgement and nerve for, at the upper end of the grades, individual moves can be difficult, the exposure great and the consequences of a fall fatal. Most of us prefer the company of a friend and a rope on harder routes, in which case our rope work, to 'pitch' safely or move together on a shortened rope, needs to be as good as that of the rock climber or the mountaineer.

Birkness Comb rising to the south of Buttermere is a wild and rocky ice-cut hollow, cradled between the ridges of High Stile and High Crag. Within this delightful bowl can be found a climbing playground, surprisingly overlooked by the first wave of lakeland explorers. It was not until the early 1900s that the first forays were made onto Eagle Crag and Grey Crag. Left dormant for much of the decade that followed, it was climber and artist Bill Peascod who made Birkness his own in the 1940s whilst preparing a guide to the area for the Fell and Rock Climbing Club.

Two easy climbs listed in that guide, Harrow

Buttress (1912) and Chockstone Ridge (1914), when followed on a warm dry day provide one of the most enjoyable scrambles in the district. They link a clean and continuous line of rough rock up three tiers of Grey Crag; a combination of slabs, blocks and pinnacles that make it feel almost Alpine in character. By avoiding the hardest pitches (the direct start up the open-book corner and the upper chimney of Chockstone Ridge) the route remains a scramble, albeit at the top of the grade. By including them, their levels of difficulty change this scramble into a rock climb of moderate difficulty, an ideal first climb for anyone with sound ropework and the judgement to undertake it.

By finishing the scramble with a round of High Crag, Hay Stacks and Fleetwith Pike you can be assured of a grand day out. Should you run out of time and energy, the route can be cut short at Scarth Gap or at the head of Warnscale Beck.

HARROW BUTTRESS
From Gatesgarth the path heading south-west to Birkness Comb follows the Scarth Gap path initially, before skirting below the ruddy rocks of Low Crag to ascend a rocky path to boggy ground close to Comb Beck. Cross the mountain wall by a ladder stile and continue into the moraine-filled and often boggy hollow of the combe. Ahead is the dark bulk of Eagle

Bill and Margaret Freeland on the pinnacle of Chockstone Ridge

Crag and high up to the right the lighter rocks of Grey Crag. Climb scree to reach the toe of the lowest rocks: this is Harrow Buttress. For those with rock-climbing experience, it can be climbed direct up the obvious corner, which leads after 9m (30ft) to a chimney and a more open corner, ending at a scoop. In all it comprises 40m (130ft) of 'moderately difficult' climbing leading to the top of Harrow Buttress. It can be avoided by venturing along a gully on the right – the scramblers' option – which leads without difficulty to the top of the buttress.

Continue on the right up a rocky edge leading in steps to the top of the arête where a perched block marks the end of the first section of scrambling. The position is superb. By descending a gully you reach the foot of Chockstone Ridge, to the right of an area of slabs scarred by a rockfall and a grassy gully.

CHOCKSTONE RIDGE

From the foot of the ridge climb a number of awkward steps to the foot of a rock needle. Climb this and from a block step airily across the chockstone-filled gap to regain the main ridge, continuing to the foot of a final superb chimney. The chimney sports good holds leading to an exit on the left, but it crosses the divide into climbing. Fortunately, there is another exit: the ledge at the foot of the chimney leads to a grassy gully on the left.

An unusual view of Birkness Comb, Grey Crag and High Seat above Buttermere

Scramble up this to a chockstone which can be passed by a ledge on the right. This leads to a grassy terrace below the final section of Grey Crag, guarded by a line of rocky gendarmes. On the left there is an obvious gap between two towers blocked by a chockstone. Climb into the gap behind the blocks and scramble up to the right, following a boulder-filled gully to reach the skyline ridge on the right. Follow this to the top where the view opens out towards Red Pike and Pillar across Ennerdale.

The rocks of Grey Crag are rough and clean and will undoubtedly draw you back, but the round leads on from the summit of High Stile south-east, skirting the rocky crest of Comb Crags and White Cove to the top of High Crag. A loose, well worn path leads down to a col and a short rise to Seat before the path descends to Scarth Gap. Here there is a choice to be made: turn left and Buttermere is half an hour away; continue on and in the same time you can be crossing the knobbly summits of Hay Stacks to Innominate Tarn and pay your respects to Alf Wainwright, whose ashes were spread close by. To take in all the summits on the Warnscale Round, as I call it, makes a really grand day out. In fact, on the way to Brandreth and Grey Knotts you pass the aptly named Great Round How. But if you run out of time, or legs, follow the path to Blackbeck Tarn and skirt Green Crag to gain the path that descends Warnscale Beck. Of course, Fleetwith Pike is a good summit and the descent down Fleetwith Edge to Gatesgarth is a marvellous way to finish the day.

Route 10: LORTON GULLY, GRASMOOR, AND A ROUND OF HOPEGILL HEAD AND WHITESIDE

	1	2	3
grade			*
quality			
navigation			

ASSESSMENT: A steep, contrasting gill scramble, at times enclosed, at times exposed, finishing with a flourish up rocky ridge and a round that includes some of the best bits of ridge walking in the area.

GRADE NOTE: Serious in wet conditions: difficulties are avoidable, but not always escapable without retreat
OS MAP: Outdoor Leisure 4
GR: 159208
DISTANCE: 9km (5.5 miles) with plenty of climbing to Grasmoor

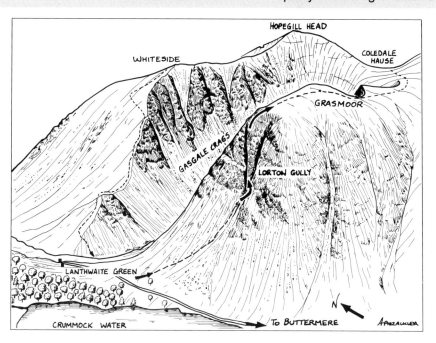

The brooding bulk of Grasmoor dominates the sward of Lanthwaite Green and the entrance to Gasgale Gill at the northern end of Crummock Water. The fell itself is not immediately attractive to the walker; its flanks are steep and uncompromising, clothed in grass, bracken and heather with few paths. But look again at the front face overlooking the road and you will see that it is cut by Y-shaped Lorton Gully. Like so many names hereabouts, Lorton is a mixture of old English and Norse and is probably derived from the name Hlora, a female found in Norse mythology. Gasgale is also old Norse, meaning 'a ravine where there are goat herders' huts'. Indeed, if you look at the OS map (GR: 160211) the circular site of an ancient homestead is marked and the route through the gill over Coledale Hause into Coledale itself is a natural route way connecting the settlements around Crummock with Braithwaite and Keswick.

Scrambling up Lorton Gully presents no route-finding difficulties; the way is well marked and obvious. The line of the scramble can best be seen from the parking place close to Lanthwaite Green Farm (GR: 158207). Initially it climbs the obvious gully with a crux below where the gully divides. Our route then scrambles up the left arm (looking up) of the 'Y' and, in the

Descending from Whiteside to Whin Ben and Crummock Water

upper section, the rocky ridge bounding its left side. The ascent of Lorton Gully to Grasmoor summit and a round of the ridge running to Coledale Hause, Hopegill Head and the superb ridge of Whiteside makes a splendid high-level traverse.

The last time I did the gully, the local hunt and its followers were out. Undeterred we set off up the steep hillside, zigzagging up scree on an ill-defined trod that seemed to be going in the direction of the gully. Before we had reached the scrambling a pack of hounds sniffed us out, soon followed by striding 'pink' huntsmen who called them in and set them off quartering the hillside in search of 'Charlie'.

Although well marked the gill is quite shallow to begin with, presenting little more than a series of clean rocky slabs and steps buried in a thicket of heather and dwarf trees. In dry conditions the route is superb; in the wet it becomes a monster and is best left alone unless you are looking for an epic. As you climb, the gully becomes more pronounced with steeper steps and narrow chimney-like sections where trees provide ample anchors for those resorting to the rope. Easier scrambling up a wider bay leads to a crux where the gully deepens, offering no escape to the left or the right. The difficulties rise in a series of steps, first up water-worn slabs then a narrow, awkward chimney followed by a final steep rise leading to easier ground at a point where the arms of the 'Y' divide.

Escape can now be found to the left and the right, but if you have come this far there is no reason not to continue. Traverse diagonally leftwards below the steep entry to the left-hand gully. Do not try to enter it directly but climb more broken ground to the left and rejoin it above a steep corner by traversing slabs of broken rock, taking care not to dislodge any loose material. Scramble up a series of enjoyable steps until the ground above eases. The best route is now to be found on the left by gaining the rocky skyline ridge which rises in a series of delightful steps ending on a rocky prow at the top of the North West Ridge. A path continues up to the top of Grasmoor.

Continue over the summit skirting Dove Crags to pick up a ridge line heading north-east towards Coledale Hause. The views towards Skiddaw are superb and if you have had enough there is a fast way back down impressive Gasgale Gill and Liza Beck to Lanthwaite Green.

However, if you have energy to spare, head north up Sand Hill to Hopegill Head for some of the loveliest ridge walking in the district. Hopegill Head is a fine summit with stunning views towards the northern fells. From its top a trilogy of ridges radiate north, east and west, all worth walking. But our return is along the narrow crest of the western arm of Whiteside; an edge as good as Striding and far less frequented. Looking west you can see the sea, the sun and, alas, the smoking towers of Sellafield. Be sure to follow the track that descends south-west towards Whin Ben and Liza Beck, and back to Lanthwaite Green.

A perfect winter's day on Whiteside with the sea and Sellafield in the distance

Route 11: LAUNCHY GILL, THIRLMERE, WITH DOB GILL
AND A ROUND OF TARNS

	1	2	3
grade (Launchy Gill)			*
grade (Dob Gill)			
quality			
navigation			

ASSESSMENT: A classic gill scramble of considerable interest, beauty, and difficulty that is best done in drier conditions. It can be followed by an interesting round of tarns and pools on the Wythburn Fells, providing a good test of map reading and navigational skill.

GRADE NOTE: Launchy Gill 3S if climbed direct
GR: 309158; or near Dobgill Bridge 316140
OS MAP: Outdoor Leisure 4
DISTANCE: 7km (4.5 miles) but hard tramping when boggy

Dark-forested Thirlmere is well fed by sparkling torrents, which is just as well for the Lake District as the throats of Manchester may have demanded more water and dammed even more of its lovely valleys had they become dry. As it is, Thirlmere seems the least offensive of those that have been lost, but the barrier of walls and wire-topped fences that have been built since the first stone was laid in 1890, by Alderman Knight, are a disgrace.

Its gills, on the other hand, are something else; a real Lake District speciality. Like the local tradition of giving rum butter to nursing mothers, they are rich and sustaining. Thirlmere's gills, in particular, are full of interest and adventure, totally disproportionate to their size. There are lots of gills, too, with Launchy Gill amongst the best, vying with Mill Gill for interest and beauty, in my opinion.

The fells on the western side of Thirlmere, unlike the loftier Helvellyn flank, provide a boggy watershed between the reservoir and Derwent Water. About half way down the west side of the reservoir, Launchy Gill thunders from the fell between Deergarth How Island and Hawes How Island, cutting through a band of steep volcanic rock. Hidden deep in the forestry plantation, its course is criss-crossed by a well constructed nature trail, reminiscent of a Victorian walkway, yet still it manages to guard its secrets from the casual observer.

Like most gills, its best to wait for drier weather

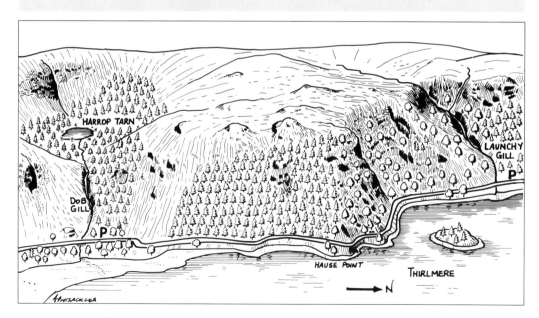

before venturing up, if patience and old age allow. In wetter conditions some of the most interesting sections become impossible to climb and staying dry is neither an option nor a probability. Unfortunately in mid-summer, when the water is low, the midge count is high and the terrain hereabouts, a mixture of bog, forest and bracken, provides the ideal breeding ground for a species of insect every bit(e) as vicious as its Scottish cousin.

LAUNCHY GILL

Launchy Gill begins its descent on the waterlogged fell below Middle Crag and Shivery Man. Flowing southwards at first, it is then turned eastwards by the rocks of Bell Crags to fall almost 185m down a rocky bed to the waters of Thirlmere. You can approach the start from either end of the lake and park by the road close to where the stream joins Manchester's drinking water.

A gate on the lake side of the road provides easy access to the stream. Pass under the bridge; if you can do this dry shod it is a fair indication of things ahead. The scrambling begins quite dramatically 100m or so upstream where the river turns a right angle into a narrow channel. This is most probably a fault line; a natural weakness followed and etched more deeply by the stream. Climb the rocky left-side of the cut above a deep pool. Ahead is a

Poised above a deep slash pool at the start of Launchy Gill

cascade with a pleasant slab on its left side; climb this on comforting holds. Beyond this cascade the stream bed is frilled with boulders and the difficulty eases, soon leading to a point where a forest trail crosses the stream by a footbridge.

Continue in the stream bed, staying on the left side, although if it becomes too difficult or the water is too high an escape can be made out left. If conditions allow, follow the stream to the base of a slab which provides some interest. Above the slab there is a deep pool and one of the crux sections on the 'direct' route. Cross to the right side of the pool somehow, but certainly not dry. You can then regain the left side and continue to the next large waterfall. It is possible to traverse the left side along a rock ledge quite high above the water. When I last did the gill a fallen tree at this point allowed us to rig a back rope. Whatever you do, the water will pluck at your heels. Beyond the pool another higher fall held between black walls provides yet more interest. Traverse in on the left along an obvious ledge. Above to the left there is a secondary water channel. Climb steeply up to this on good incut holds, moving right at an obvious rock spike. A difficult step lets you reach easier ground, albeit in an exposed position, and climb directly up the secondary channel.

Beyond this difficult section the way relents for a while. Continue along the left side until it

Swinging above the thundering force of Launchy Gill with too much water

is possible to boulder-hop to the other side. Ahead is a narrow ravine. Traverse a good footledge along its right wall to reach a deep plunge pool below an impressive fall. Traverse around the pool on the right and escape up trees and vegetation on the right of the cascade.

Above this fall the stream divides into two channels, the one on the right being the smallest and favourite. Scramble up this by way of a series of rock steps contained in a dark and slippery ravine which leads at last to the end of the scrambling. The main stream continues to a final impressive fall offering little in the way of easy scrambling. A grassy gully on the left leads unsatisfactorily to the trees and the edge of the plantation.

There is still a lot left of Launchy Gill but alas the barrier of crags that provided the rocky interest runs out, whilst ahead lies more gentle terrain, but not without interest. Launchy Tarn, not marked but named on the OS map, is really a widening of the gill that fills a shallow peaty hollow, not a tarn at all. Not far away, to the south, there is another well marked tarn on the same map! A route to the tarns leads via the outcrops of Bell Crag and to a disused quarry. To the south-east of the working are two more tiny pools well worth a visit, if only to test your navigation. The last time I covered this ground there were three herons fishing the beautiful clear water of Launchy Gill where the tarn should be, and a group of twelve hinds on the skyline crags near Stone Hause.

Just over the rise are the dark, open waters

Looking across Thirlmere towards Blencathra from the forest surrounding Launchy Gill

of Blea Tarn, by far the most important on these fells. No matter at what time of the year I visit this area, I'm always surprised by how few walkers I meet. A few venture from Watendlath as far as the tarn but not far beyond, despite the fact that a good track crosses the fell to Wythburn. From Blea Tarn make your way to Standing Crag by way of two more peaty pools. The crag itself has a lot of rock and provides some interesting problems. As a final test of your skill with a map, try to find the tiny jewels of water in a peaty basin south of the crag.

If Ullscarf's summit holds no mystery for you return northwards from Standing Crag, picking up the streams that form Mosshause Gill to the east. A track descends through dark plantations to reed-bound Harrop Tarn. This is a lovely tarn, dappled on a warm summer's evening with the pools of rising trout and the pink reflection of bulky Helvellyn across the valley.

DOB GILL

Issuing from Harrop Tarn is Dob Gill which provides an interesting finale to this watery round. Essentially a boulder-filled stream bed, it is nevertheless an attractive watercourse that provides some easy scrambling both in descent and ascent. Simply descend the rocky gill bed to the road, from where it is a short but delightful walk along the lakeside to Launchy Gill.

Route 12: PILLAR ROCK BY THE SLAB AND NOTCH ROUTE

	1	2	3
grade			*
quality			
navigation			

ASSESSMENT: A Lake District classic, steeped in history, to one of the most inaccessible summits in the country.

GRADE NOTE: slightly easier if the 'Easy Way' variation is taken: the same way is taken in descent

OS MAP: Outdoor Leisure 4
GR: 195150, Gatesgarth Farm, Buttermere; 186088, Wasdale Head
DISTANCE: 11km (7 miles) with a lot of ascent and descent

There are few summits in England from which the adventurous walker is excluded but Pillar Rock is definitely one. Fewer still are the summits whose first ascent is as accurately recorded as that of the Rock. On 9 July 1826, one John Atkinson, cooper and shepherd of Croftfoot, Ennerdale, climbed alone to the summit, probably by what is now known as 'The Old West'. Others followed; most were shepherds with a knowledge of the 'Pillar Stone', as it was locally known, gained from searching for crag-bound sheep.

Between Atkinson's ascent in 1826 and 1860 it is estimated that only six parties reached the top. One was led by C.A.O. Baumgartner who is also credited with the first traverse of airy Crib Goch. Swiss by birth, he was bagging firsts in Britain whilst members of the Alpine Club were busy potting unclimbed Alpine peaks. The first female ascent was made in 1870 by Miss A. Barker.

Without doubt, an ascent of Pillar Rock is a must for any lakeland scrambler. But do not underestimate the feat. The route described (Slab and Notch) is a journey into climbing history. Although not difficult, the route is exposed and serious, demanding route-finding skills. The same route is also followed in descent when a rope is essential to protect the party. First climbed in August 1861 by a party of five led by the Keeper of the St Bees lighthouse, it is not known whether they took the 'Easy Way' variation. Whatever, it remains the most popular

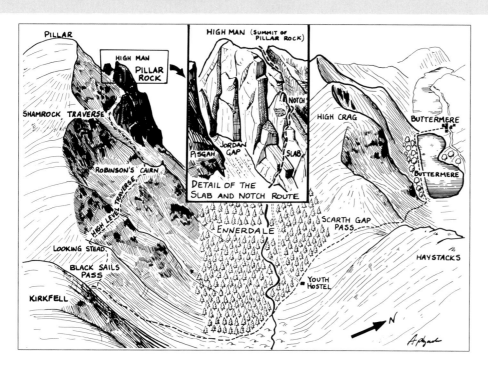

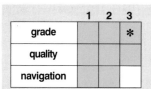

scrambling route and the usual route of descent for climbers.

There are many ways to approach Pillar Rock, the most obvious being by way of Ennerdale. Those based in Wasdale should make the haul to Black Sail Pass and join the 'High-Level Route' into the Rock. This spectacular footpath traverses a precipitous fellside to Pillar Rock and was discovered by John Wilson Robinson, an early Pillarite. Further along the path a large cairn, Robinson's Cairn, has been built as a memorial to the man. To make a good day of it, a sporting return to Wasdale is by way of Pillar, Wind Gap and Red Pike. Of course, there is always the option of a speedy return down Mosedale, if it looks as though you will miss 'last orders'.

Because I normally approach from the north my usual starting point is Gatesgarth Farm in Buttermere. The first leg south to Scarth Gap is a bit of a haul, but your efforts are soon rewarded by a view to the Gables or down dark-forested Ennerdale. There is a direct approach to the foot of Pillar Rock, seen high on the opposite side of the valley, but this avoids the classic High-Level Route pioneered by Robinson. For me it remains the most impressive way to become acquainted with the Rock. Descend south-west to tiny Black Sail Youth Hostel and ascend the path besides Sail Beck to the pass. From here take the path over

Traversing the easy but exposed slab on Pillar's classic Slab and Notch

Exposed, easy scrambling to the summit having rounded the Notch

the lesser summit of Pisgah. From Robinson's Cairn continue into Pillar Cove and follow Shamrock Traverse, a steeply inclined shelf leading towards the gap separating Pisgah from Pillar mountain. Before you reach this gap a small cairn marks a traverse below Pisgah to the gully leading to the Jordan Gap. From this point the slab of Slab and Notch is on the right of the gully.

The slab is set at an easy angle but beware – it lies above a steep and exposed crag. Gain the slab by scrambling up a short steep wall on good holds or by a crack on the right. Now descend the slab and gain a ledge leading rightwards to below a small pinnacle. From here gain the Notch between this tower and the main face by scrambling up a steep, exposed corner. From the Notch a ledge leads right where easier scrambling on good holds leads upwards and further right into a gully (Great Chimney). Easy scrambling leads to the top.

The climb to the Notch can be avoided by the 'Easy Way' which traverses right around a nose at the base of the 'tower' rather than directly to the Notch. Easy but exposed ledges lead downwards slightly to gain the easy upper section of the Great Chimney. In descent, either of these routes can be followed.

In all, this gives little more than 45m of scrambling, which may not seem a lot compared to the amount of hard walking needed to reach it. But quality not quantity is what this one is all about, and remember – it welcomes you into the exclusive society of Pillarites.

Looking Stead and turn right to join the High-Level Route.

By the time you reach Robinson's cairn on the far side of Hind Cove, Pillar Rock rises impressively ahead of you. Take time to spy out the way. The highest point of Pillar Rock is High Man. To the south of this is a deep cleft known as the Jordan Gap, beyond which is

Route 13: FAIRFIELD BY WAY OF LINK COVE GILL AND GREENHOW END SLABS

	1	2	3
grade (Link Cove Gill)		*	
grade (Green 'Low End)			
quality			
navigation			

ASSESSMENT: High-quality gill scrambling followed by an open and exposed buttress route that leads to the fell top and a fine walk down open ridge country.

OS MAP: Outdoor Leisure 5
GR: 399144, small lay-by at Bridgend
DISTANCE: 11km (7 miles) via Fairfield and Hart Crag

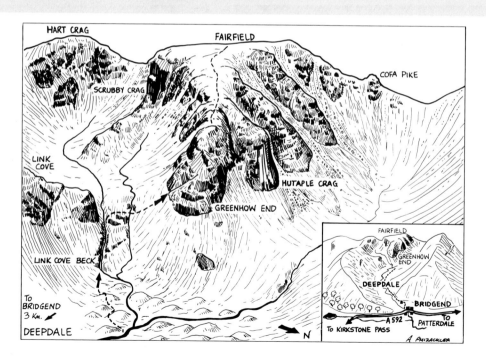

Patterdale, the St Patrick's end of sinuous Ullswater, is the starting point of many fine walks and scrambles. This one is no exception. The ascent of well named Fairfield from Bridgend by way of Deepdale, and a scramble up the gill draining Link Cove and the slabs of Greenhow End, offers a contrasting and enjoyable route to the top. Harry Griffin first drew my attention to it, a route worthy of this doyen of lakeland fells. In all it provides a delightful mixture of scrambling and open ridge walking with extensive views, on a good day, from Helvellyn to Scafell, with the lakes of Grasmere and Windermere like sheets of silver to the south.

South of Patterdale on the A592, just beyond the crag named after the son of Arni, probably a Viking farmer, the road crosses Deepdale Beck at Bridgend. A lay-by alongside the telephone box provides parking and the starting point for this round.

Go back over the bridge then follow the farm track to Wallend and continue south-east along the footpath into Deepdale. The farm buildings here are well built, as is the packhorse bridge by the last of them. The track rises gently to provide an enjoyable route towards Sleet Cove and Deepdale Hause. Ahead, the valley changes; rough Nature and the deposition of glaciers taking over from nurture. Before the

Sallie O'Connor in action on the delightful slab on Greenhow End, high above Deepdale

path climbs to the hause take a less-worn trod through hummocky moraines leading leftwards alongside the gurgling gill that cascades from Link Cove by way of a deep cut cleft; the line of the scramble. The haunt of wagtail and dipper, Deepdale seems curiously neglected in favour of nearby tourist haunts of Grisedale and Dovedale.

The exercise of putting hands to rock begins at the rough slabs left of the first waterfall. This is followed by a bout of boulder-hopping and provides a pleasant prelude to what follows. The gill now rises in a series of fine cascades, not all of which can be climbed. The first major obstacle has always stopped me, but thankfully the slabby arête on the right provides a worthy alternative and leads by way of an exposed traverse back to the bed of the stream above the impasse. The state of the water will invariably dictate the route. In optimum conditions it is possible to stay dry by bridging widely to avoid the stream, or else traversing delicately along its sidewalls, balancing on the stream-cleaned rock in favour of the treacherous, lichened alternative and the sucking pools below. Having overcome a series of intricate problems and small falls, onward progress is barred by a major force. Twelve metres or so above , the stream pours through a narrow cleft before cascading over a barrier of slabs. The best scrambling is on the left of the stream below an overhanging tree up a series of water-worn and lichened steps. Although it is easy to escape left, a traverse rightwards beneath the tree provides a purist's exit through the cleft. The way ahead now opens out although there is still more scrambling to be had, first in the gill bed and then on the right up a rocky arête bounding the stream. The last time we did this round, on a hot July day, the pool above the cascade provided a cooling dip before slogging on to the slabs above.

GREENHOW END SLABS

Greenhow End, the continuation of our route can be seen on the right, a rocky buttress, below The Step, truncating the ridge thrown down from Fairfield. Traverse towards the lowest rocks on the left side, crossing a shallow gully and bouldery scree before you reach the toe of a rib of rough, dark rock. This is below a grass rake, 15m (49ft) or so up the hill, that runs diagonally rightwards, providing a steep walker's path which is cairned. Climb the rib, moving right at its top to gain a grass terrace below a steeper wall. Walk left below this band of black slabs to follow a weakness climbed first to the right and then back left and finally rightwards to make an exit by an obvious block to reach easier ground which connects with the grass rake, the walker's route mentioned earlier. Cross the rake and scramble up an easy-angled, water-worn, open-book corner. Continue for a while up easy slabs on coarse volcanic rock, as abrasive as pumice. Cross a shallow gully on the right to reach another rock rib and yet more slabs which are followed until the level eases and the scrambling runs out. A faint path leads more or less over The Step across curiously named Black Tippet and Flinty Grave to meet the main path between Hart Crag and Fairfield's summit.

There are plenty of options for the return leg. The quickest route is by way of Deepdale Hause to the north, where a well marked path leads into Sleet Cove, beneath Hutaple Crag, descending the 4.5km (2.8 miles) or so to Bridgend down aptly named Deepdale.

A more enjoyable round is to retrace your steps to Link Hause and continuing the climb to Hart Crag before turning sharply eastwards along the fine ridge separating Deepdale from Dovedale. This narrowing crest drops between Erne Nest Crag and Black Crag before levelling out by Hartsop above How. The footpath descends more gently here, following the mountain wall along the crest of the spur before dropping into the woods of Deepdale Park where a marked track leads back to the lay-by at Bridgend.

Entering the deep cleft of Link Cove Beck

Route 14: MILL GILL AND THE DODDS, ST JOHN'S IN THE VALE

	1	2	3
grade			*
quality			
navigation			

ASSESSMENT: A hidden gill scramble that is surprisingly long with some difficult pitches; best done in dry conditions. Taking a rope is advised.

OS MAP: Outdoor Leisure 5
GR: 318196, Legburthwaite car park
DISTANCE: 8km (5 miles) via Watson's Dodd and Stake Pass

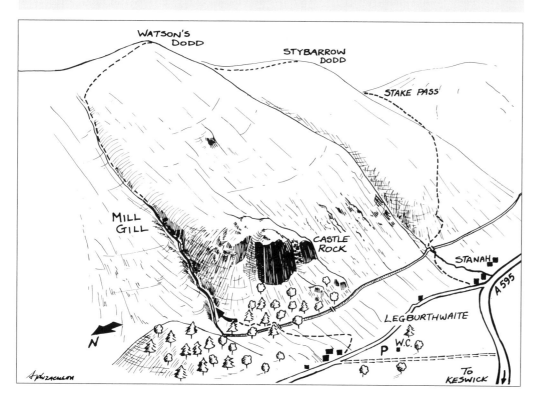

The southern portal of St John's in the Vale is dominated by the massive ramparts of romantically named Castle Rock of Triemain, rising like a natural fortress to guard the passage from broader Thirlmere. The steep eastern flank of this narrow vale boasts a clutch of steep, deep ravines that cascade off the Dodds to provide some of the most entertaining scrambles in the Lakes. Mill Gill, just north of Castle Rock, which drains the ground between Great Dodd and Watson's Dodd, is one of the finest and longest, with over 450m (1476ft) of vertical gain.

It is hard to imagine a scramble which is easier to reach than Mill Gill, so it is surprising that it does not get more traffic. There is even easy parking at Legburthwaite below Castle Rock off the A591. This route offers thought-provoking work in a deep cleft. What is more, with continuous interest, it provides a delightful way to the summit of Great Dodd.

The naming of Castle Rock, like many sites in the northern lakes and the Eden Valley, has close links with ancient Britain and Arthurian legend. A local story has it that King Arthur, the immortal hero of Royal Britain, whose veins coursed with the blood of the lineage of Vortigern, was, as we all know, the son of Uter Pendragon whose castle still stands in the Eden Valley. Arthur, having built the Round Table by Eamont Bridge on the A6, staged a great tournament, promising the hand of his natural daughter Gwyneth to the most valiant knight. It seems that the lass caused too many to bite

the dust, forcing Merlin to intervene by placing a spell on the lovely Gwyneth, after which he took her off to the Castle Rock where she fell into a deep sleep. After 500 years the valiant Sir Roland de Vaux, the Baron of Triemain, by overcoming the four temptations of fear, avarice, pleasure and ambition, was able to break the spell and claim her hand. I wonder what temptations the modern knight has to overcome in order to claim Mill Gill; certainly fear, pleasure and ambition will play their part.

From the car park follow the track through fields into a plantation below the Castle Rock. Cross the Thirlmere Aqueduct, a leat that feeds the lake, and follow a trod to the stream bed on the left. I have in the past, for the sake of purity, started Mill Gill at the road, making my way under bridges, through the mill, over debris and a dead deer to follow its entire course to the summit of the Great Dodd.

From below, the delights of Mill Gill are hidden from the ambitious but that is true of most lakeland watercourses. This scramble is best done after a dryish spell as the gorge is narrow with cascades that are impassable in wet weather. Even in dry conditions, following the direct route presents considerable difficulty and fear will play its part; a rope is certainly advised.

Guarding entry to the deep recesses of the first ravine is a cascade which is climbed on the right. If you get a soaking here, passing

Bill Freeland in the lost world of lush vegetation low down the Gill

71

this small fall successfully on the route ahead is unlikely. Follow the bed of the gill until your way is blocked by another waterfall and you are forced to pass it by climbing out of the ravine on the right and so regain the gill above the impasse.

Continue on the right-hand side of the stream by traversing the sidewall, using a tree root as a handrail. Above another small fall, cross slippery rocks to the left-hand side of the stream and continue to where the gorge widens. The vegetation, overhanging trees, lichened rock and rushing water all combine to make this an impressive place. Follow the stream to where it divides and follow the left-hand branch to where the angle eases considerably.

Just when you think the best may be over and your ambition has been realised, the gill is channelled through another ravine. The initial problems are merely a warm-up for what follows. Easy scrambling leads to a vertical fall tumbling into a deep pool. The wall on the left provides a tricky solution. A foothold on the slab allows you to bridge out onto a small hold on the right. A root provides a handhold, allowing you to straddle higher on the left wall and so gain a small sapling. All the while the deep pool and the fear of falling are sucking at your heels. Swing up right and the problem is passed. Fail and you take a bath!

Ahead the gill divides as it cascades over yet another fall. Reach this on the right where a number of sharp-cut holds lead improbably up a steep vegetative wall. Continue by overcoming a delightful series of problems in the gorge until it narrows yet again and the way ahead looks difficult. Cross to the right-hand side of the stream and climb up to a jammed block where there is a natural arch. Depending on the amount of water, either swing out left or crawl through the hole. Either way you are unlikely to remain dry!

If you have got this far, the way ahead should present no great problems, although there is still plenty of interest. In particular, a cascade to the left of an overhung block presents a problem in wet conditions and is best overcome by a difficult traverse of the left wall. This is soon followed by the last major step, yet another cascade, which can be passed on the left by an awkward move to pass a block. This gives access to wet slabs and an exposed step that leads to easier ground.

There are still small problems to overcome, but no more major ones. By following the stream you eventually climb out high on the grassy slopes of Great Dodd from where a round over Watson's Dodd and Stybarrow Dodd to Sticks Pass to the south leads to a footpath back to Legburthwaite.

Steep traversing on the right wall of Mill Gill

Route 15: Helvellyn Gill and Browncove Crags

	1	2	3
grade (Helvellyn Gill)	*		
grade (Browncove Crags)		*	
quality			
navigation			

ASSESSMENT: Contrasting scrambles; an enclosed uncomplicated gill followed by an exposed crag, with intricate route-finding that leads to Lower Man and Helvellyn.

OS MAP: Outdoor Leisure 5
GR: 316168, National Trust car park
DISTANCE: 13km (8 miles) via Nethermost and Grisedale Tarn

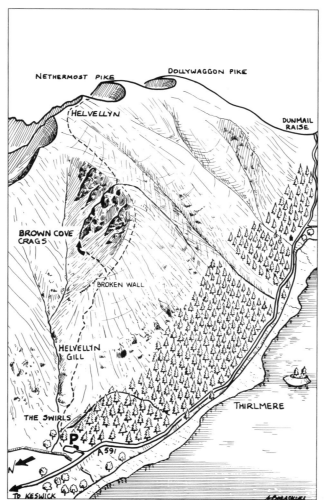

The Thirlmere flank of Helvellyn, between Dunmail Raise to the south and the pub at Thirlspot to the north, seems at first glance a monotonous fellside with little to interest the scrambler. It does not stand comparison with the mountain's eastern flank; all ridges, rocks and precipitous coves. But take a closer look at the map and you will notice two redeeming features. First, this monotonous slope provides a large number of streams to slake the needs of thirsty Manchester and, second, on the shoulder of Lower Man, there is a rocky buttress marked Browncove Crags on the map. Fortunately for the scrambler this provides some interesting and intricate rock that redeems the day. Doubly fortunate, the stream below it, Helvellyn Gill, provides a much more enjoyable alternative to the footpath that is a trade-route to Helvellyn and leads almost to the base of the crag.

From the car park at Highpark Wood you can engage the gill immediately, but it is better to cross the wooden bridge and walk the path as far as the next before entering the bouldery stream bed.

Helvellyn Gill and Browncove Crags

The scrambling in Helvellyn Gill is neither steep nor continuous but it does offer a series of small, albeit avoidable, problems that provide a warm-up before the serious business of Browncove Crags. There is little to say about the route-finding; it is all too obvious and in all but very wet conditions you should find it enjoyable. There are several small falls *enroute* that provide the testing bits and it proves difficult to pass a well jammed boulder without a little dampness – but that is the nature of gill scrambling. Eventually the interest gives out around the 500m (1640ft) contour close to a point where a ruined dry stone wall strikes up the hillside towards Browncove Crags.

Follow this wall or the path close by until you can traverse awkward scree to the base of the lowest rocks of the crag. There are plenty of possibilities here for the experienced scrambler and I have never followed the same route twice.

From the lowest rocks a ramp can be followed diagonally leftwards until the slabs above can be followed towards a terrace and an obvious chimney bridged by a massive jammed boulder. Climbed direct, the chimney is awkward. Alternatively, a vegetative rake leads up to the left into a basin below a steep section of crag, with an obvious steep corner left of centre.

In order to go upwards and onwards there are now several choices. Traverse right across easy ledges and you reach the edge of the crag and can scramble upwards to the top of this steep step. Alternatively, you can cross a slab to the right, below the steep corner, and climb broken ground below it to gain a grassy ledge which runs leftwards from its base to the edge of the buttress. This same spot can be reached by climbing an obvious wide crack up the left side of the buttress. More broken ground now leads upwards by way of terraces and vegetation to the base of a ridge, forming the skyline

above and to the right. Follow this ridge and continue to the top of the buttress. The normal footpath is further to the right. In poor visibility the route is not easy to find, but there are plenty of alternatives and in wet conditions the rocks, being north-facing, are lichened and slimy.

Having milked the climbable rock to the full, you arrive close to Lower Man where the main path swings around Brown Cove, on the south side of the ridge, towards the top of Swirral Edge. Continue over the top of Helvellyn

Intricate route finding on Browncove Crags

decorated with a trig, shelter wall and memorial, and follow the path south around Nethermost Cove to its Pike. There is a path that descends, via Birk Side, to Thirlmere near Wythburn. Instead, keep to the ridge and continue over High Crag to Dollywaggon Pike (whose name is an enigma) and drop to Grisedale Tarn before descending right on the path alongside Raise Beck to Dunmail Raise.

Not everybody crossing the pass of Dunmail Raise knows why the road divides on either side of a huge cairn or indeed why a cairn was raised. Local tradition has it that Dunmail, King of Strathclyde, fought a battle here in 945 against Edmund, King of the Saxons, and was killed. This was a time when Cumbria was part of the Kingdom of Strathclyde, a period which has often been recalled in heroic poems including these verses from the Victorian 'Ballad of King Dunmail' by John Pagen White.

> They buried on the mountain's side
> King Dunmail, where he fought and died.
> But mount and mere and moor again
> Shall see King Dunmail come to reign.
>
> Mantled and mailed repose his bones
> Twelve cubits deep beneath the stones;
> But many fathoms deeper down,
> In Grisedale mere lies Dunmail's crown.

It seems, however, that Dunmail fled the battle and died some 30 years later in Rome, so there is no point in retracing your steps and dredging Grisedale Tarn.

Having paid your respects, take the path on the Helvellyn side of the road, following it over footbridge and through forest back to Highpark Wood where you started the day.

Steep scrambling beside a small cascade in Helvellyn Gill

Route 16: BLENCATHRA: SHARP EDGE AND HALL'S FELL RIDGE

	1	2	3
grade (Sharp Edge)	*		
grade (Hall's Fell Ridge)			
quality			
navigation			

ASSESSMENT: Exposed ridge walking and scrambling offering some of the finest views in the northern lakes.

OS MAP: Outdoor Leisure 5
GR: 348273; or 349270, small lay-by near Scales on A66
DISTANCE: 7km (4.4 miles) steep and interesting throughout

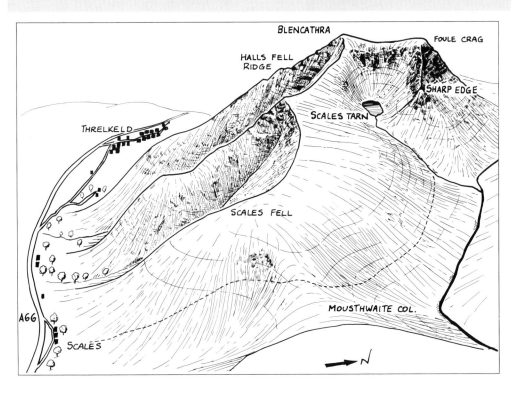

There are some splendid ridge walks in the Lakes but very little in the way of prolonged ridge scrambling that you find in Scotland and sometimes in Wales. The weather and time have long since rounded the bristling arêtes and have left us with broad-backed ridges ideal for the fell runner and striding walker. On the map there are mountains that look as though they should offer ridge scrambling but in reality there is little rock. Rarely are the arêtes narrow enough for hands and feet to come into play.

I have grown to love the Northern Fells; Souther and the back of Skiddaw have become favourite haunts when I want rough walks or need to be alone. But it is unmistakable Blencathra, rising like a wave about to break over Threlkeld Common, that attracts me most and incidentally provides one of the best ridge scrambles in the Lake District – Sharp Edge. Indeed, the combination of Sharp Edge with any of Saddleback's other ridges makes for an exposed and stimulating day on the hill.

Approached along the A66 from Penrith, this bold saddlebacked fell stands guardian over the Northern Lakes; far more a mountaineers' playground than gentle Skiddaw, as the view from the road makes plain. Not a lofty hill, it makes the most of its meagre 868m (2848ft). Its precipitous southern and eastern flanks scalloped by ice look like a giant pie crust baked to perfection and weathered by time. The whole south-east facet of Blencathra is made up of a series of rib-like ridges: Gategill Fell, Middle Tongue, Hall's Fell Ridge, Doddick Fell,

Scales Fell and, most impressive of all, Sharp Edge. These are separated by the overdeep valleys of Blease Gill, Gate Gill, Doddick Gill, Scaley Beck and Scales Beck. In fact, it is only Scales Tarn, below Sharp Edge, and the gill that tumbles from it that have the shapely hallmark of an ice-age landscape, but in reality all were carved from the slatey rock by the passage of ice. The name Blencathra, like many in Cumbria, is derived from the ancient Cymric, the language of the first Celtic settlers, the Cymry. Their legacy lives on in the many Welsh-sounding place names found in the Lakes. Blencathra probably comes from the Welsh words *blaen*, meaning summit, and *cateir*, chair. Certainly the name fits the mountain's shape, as does Saddleback, a name which first appeared around 1769.

This most accessible of lakeland mountains holds a great store of delights and can provide what for many is the best true ridge scramble in the Lakes. The round of Sharp Edge and Hall's Fell Ridge, although short, is an exciting enterprise offering fine views of the Northern Pennines and Central Fells. Whatever combination of ridges you undertake do not miss out Sharp Edge. The main difficulties, and they are not great, are concentrated in a short section where a pinnacle bars access to a gap. The fact that the rock is smooth and slatey makes this exposed spot feel precarious in

Scales Tarn with Shap Edge on the right

Blencathra well covered in winter snow

slippery conditions. Beyond the gap an open groove provides the next obstacle, which for many is the crux of the whole ridge. Under windy, wet or icy conditions it can be difficult and is a well known black spot. In descent you need to exercise great care in finding the right line from the top of the fell to the horizontal section of the ridge.

SHARP EDGE

Park on the A66 at Scales or drive past the White Horse Inn and park by Comb Beck below Mousthwaite Comb. Sharp Edge remains hidden from common view; its sharply defined ridge separates Foule Crag from Tarn Crag on Atkinson Pike, the northernmost outlier of Blencathra.

A footpath leaves the road and climbs through wet fields into Mousthwaite Comb where an old quarry track cuts steeply across

the hillside to reach the col between Scales Fell and Souther Fell. Continue along the path, contouring Scales Fell above the Glenderamackin River, another rolling name whose source is in the ancient Celtic tongue. Eventually the track, which has provided a comfortable, almost-level walk, meets cascading Scales Beck tumbling from an unseen tarn. Cross the stream and ascend more steeply on the right to reach quickly the hidden gem of Scales Tarn nestling below a semicircle of rough crags. The onward route climbs the rough track to the north leading to the smooth, angular rocks forming the toe of Sharp Edge (GR:326283). There is a path that avoids the edge by traversing below the crest on the north side. In fact, all it does is avoid the best scrambling and leaves you with an exposed and unpleasant alternative to regain the ridge. Leave it alone.

Instead, climb the ridge direct. An easy-angled open groove provides the real start and, with no great difficulty, leads up the ever-sharpening crest. In places the edge is pavement-wide, quite flat but exposed and smooth. Elsewhere small pinnacles and a sloping crest force you left or right until a final pinnacle leads awkwardly to a gap where Sharp Edge butts into the main fell. Many find the next step the crux, especially in descent. Above is a broad, slabby buttress with an open groove to the right. Either follow the groove or climb the slabs to its left. These feel exposed but good hand and footholds make them enjoyable. All too quickly the scrambling ends and you reach easier ground below Atkinson Pike. From near its summit the path leads around the head of Tarn Crags ascending slowly to the top of Blencathra. There are plenty of interesting ways off the top but Hall's Fell Ridge is probably the most in keeping with what has gone before. For an entertaining alternative, try descending one of the heather-filled canyons separating the ridges.

Hall's Fell Ridge

From the summit cairn of Blencathra, descend south-east along from Hallsfell Top down a narrow ridge. Hall's Fell is not as difficult as Sharp Edge but is nevertheless steep and exposed. Its crest can be followed, more or less, although a walking path provides easier alternatives. Eventually the scrambling gives way to knee-jarring walking down the truncated toe of the ridge. A track skirts along the base of the fell crossing, in turn, Doddick Gill and Scaley Beck. Follow this path behind Scales Farm and the White Horse Inn until it eventually reaches Comb Beck and the start of the round. If you are lucky the White Horse will be open for refreshment – remember the important saying, 'hydrate or die'.

Dave Felton on Shap Edge with Bannadale Crags beyond

Route 17: MOSEDALE BECK FORCE, SWINDALE

	1	2	3
grade		*	
quality			
navigation			

ASSESSMENT: A varied and interesting scramble amidst fine scenery in one of the quietest, least-known valleys in the Lakes.

GRADE NOTE: Plenty of harder or easier options
OS MAP: Outdoor Leisure 5
GR: 515133, limited parking.
DISTANCE: 9km (5.6 miles) via Willy Winder Hill

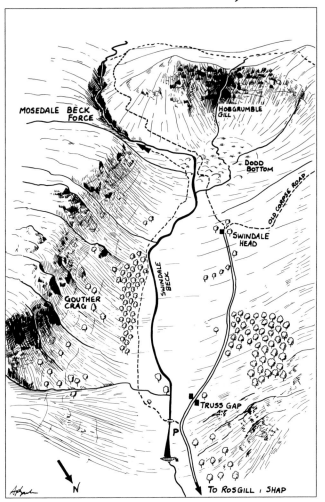

There are times when being rejected is a positive advantage. Swindale, a few miles from bleak Shap Fell, is one of a cluster of dead-end dales that form the easternmost valleys radiating from the mountainous heart of the Lake District. Like Mardale, Wet Sleddale and Longsleddale, its road simply ends, giving access to remote farms and fells. And like Mardale and Wet Sleddale, Swindale was looked at by the Manchester Corporation but, unlike them, was rejected. Even so, the burghers left their mark; a tiny chapel near Truss Farm was deconsecrated and eventually pulled down, as was the schoolroom. In return, there is an ill-kept Water Board property near the entrance to the dale that is a disgrace both to them and the National Park. Despite these blemishes on its landscape, Swindale remains my favourite haunt amongst the far eastern fells.

Swindale is only a tiny valley – you can walk its length in an hour – but there are within it countless treasures. Close to Truss Gap there is a plexus of crags with climbs to satisfy all-comers. There is interesting wildlife too; I have seen raven and peregrine as well as the eagles from neighbouring Riggindale enjoying their solitude, whilst the sound of buzzard is a constant companion when climbing on Swindale's crags. On numerous evenings on my return from the dale I've watched fell ponies and deer and even seen badger scurrying along the Water Board's road.

The far eastern fells are not renowned for scrambling. They hold few great rock buttresses

and what there are can be loose and scrappy. But these hills are home to some fine water-courses and it is these that offer the best sport. Swindale is no exception. At the head of the dale the Mosedale Beck, horseback brown, canters down rocky cascades from a peaty moor to meander amongst moraines, piled like eggs and sausages, on Swindale's floor.

For a longer day out, Swindale combines quite naturally with the scrambles up Rowantreethwaite Beck to the west which end on the Old Corpse Road and descends along it to Swindale Head from where it is an enjoyable stroll through snaking moraines to the start of the scramble up Mosedale Force. A good path then continues past Mosedale Cottage joining the Gatescarth Pass track (just onto the Outdoor Leisure map 7) from Mardale Head. A high-level route, and one I favour, contours round the head of the dale and climbs Selside, crossing to Gatescarth by way of Artlecrag Pike. Or a more interesting return from this top is down Woodfell Gill to a point around the 400m (1312ft) contour, where a break in the slope provides a descending ramp leading to Gatescarth Beck.

I normally find myself going into Swindale during long, sunny summer evenings with no intention of hurrying; Swindale does not lend itself to haste. I park at the lay-by before Truss Gap farm, crossing the beck by a convenient

Climbing around a delightful cascade in Mosedale Beck – a necklace of pools and falls

footbridge nearby to gain the path that traverses the hillside below Gouther, Dog and Outlaw crags. The track eventually recrosses the beck by a small wooden squeeze bridge at a point where the scrambling begins below Mosedale Beck Force.

In its race from Swindale Common, Mosedale Beck has cut a fine series of falls, impressive by any standard with plunge pools that have few equals. This is known as the Force, and is best attempted after a dry spell on a warm day when a swim is obligatory and sheep-cropped turf provides a comfortable bower in which to dry out and eat your sandwiches.

Scramble at first up the right side of the beck, avoiding the first pool. Easier scrambling up slabs follows left of the main stream where numerous options present themselves. A rib dividing an overflow channel from the main stream is followed and leads to steep, slippery steps. Beyond these a large fall can be passed on the right to reach an impressive plunge pool. The gorge above is quite narrow and the ground impressive. Avoid the difficulties by escaping to the sidewalls and regain the gill above this impasse. Vegetative scrambling in an exposed position allows further upward progress to continue to a point where the gill bed is strewn with slippery boulders.

Escape from the gill can now be made by traversing boulders to the right of the stream

The force of Mosedale Beck – 'horseback brown' – cantering down to Swindale

and avoiding the next fall by a high-level traverse. Continue up rocks to an impressive cascade, again marked by another fine pool. This can be overcome by traversing around the pool and climbing steeply and easily up rocks to the left.

Sadly the scramble is all too short, but is readily combined with a hike over Selside and a re-turn to Truss Gap Farm by way of the Old Corpse Road. For a longer and quite interesting walk through fell country that feels surprisingly wild, follow the path up Mosedale but instead of continuing to the cottage climb east over Scam Matthew to the head of Wet Sleddale and return to Truss Gap by way of Seat Robert, Willy Winder Hill and Black Crag.

Route 18: Hopgill Beck and Rowantreethwaite Gill, Mardale

	1	2	3
grade (Hopgill Beck)			
grade (Rowantreethwaite)			
quality			
navigation			

ASSESSMENT: The best of two complimentary gills; steep, interesting with a fair share of vegetation and slippery rock. Very worthwhile.

OS MAP: Outdoor Leisure 5
GR: 479118
DISTANCE: 3km (1.9 miles) descending the Corpse Road

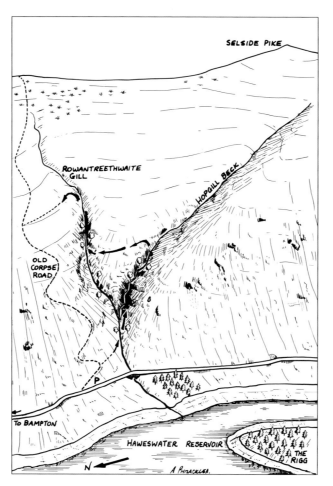

When combined, these two neighbouring gills provide an enjoyable, easily reached scramble. Close to the road they are ideal for a short day or if you intend going on to other Mardale scrambles.

Wandering across the fellside like this, I know Rowantreethwaite Gill must have felt the iron-bound clogs of Mardale shepherds. At the end of the gather or in spring after a heavy winter, you can imagine man and dog searching the likely places for lost sheep. The gills form a natural fold in bad weather but their rocks are slippery and precipitous and anyone familiar with lakeland's gills instantly recognises the stench of a bloated Herdwick that has lost its footing.

Rowantreethwaite Gill has a wonderful view-point; just turn around and look about. Its steep sidewalls act like blinkers, defining the view and drawing your eye towards The Rigg jutting into Haweswater. The shepherd must have looked down on his home at its foot and considered it permanent, as solid as the rock on which it was built. It would have seemed unimaginable that a village, its homes, pub and ancient church, founded by Norsemen, could or would be destroyed by people in Manchester, a place he had probably never seen. But the fact of the matter is this: the dam was built, the church removed, the homes destroyed and the valley submerged. It is only at times of drought that the sad ruins are revealed and we

are reminded to be on our guard for what is left of our wild country, even that within our National Parks.

HOPGILL BECK

Parking is difficult in Mardale, but there are places close to the Old Corpse Road, along which the local dead were taken on the backs of fell ponies to Shap for burial. The start of this scramble begins 90m or so along the new road towards the dale head where the stream is crossed. There is a bit of space for parking here as well.

Go through the gate where at once you are in the stream bed. Follow it, climbing through low branches to gain the smaller cascade joining the main Rowantreethwaite stream from a narrow cleft on the right; this is Hopgill Beck. Scramble towards the cleft, avoiding the pool on the right, and climb with some difficulty but with good holds up the steep wall on the right. The cleft is green and verdant, as will be obvious when you get to grips with the next two falls which are best passed on the left. Beyond them is a third and stiffer cascade marked by a jammed block which is also passed on the left, allowing you to regain the stream bed where another pool and fall are easily passed. Soon the stream bends right to emerge

At the start of the interesting scrambling in Hopgill Beck

from the dark, narrow cleft, providing a chance to look around.

Continue following the now more open gill using slabs on the left side. Avoid the steep wall by bearing right before gaining the left-hand channel beyond. The mossy cascade above is best passed on the right to gain access to another plunge pool and the continuation of the water course until slabs lead to a large tree.

ROWNTREETHWAITE GILL

At this point the scramble up Hopgill has run parallel to Rowentreethwaite over on the left, but you have not missed much in the way of scrambling as the best is to be found in the upper section. To reach it, follow a vague trod leftwards across the hillside and descend by way of steep grass to the gill bed.

Now continue up the gill which is only really practicable in dry conditions. Climb more or less directly up the best sections of rock, resorting to convenient tree roots when the handholds run out. These problems lead eventually to the final fall. The crux of the scramble is a groove to the right of the stream which proves quite awkward but leads to easier ground and the fellside where a sheep trod traverses the hill to join the Old Corpse Road above the zigzags.

Snowcapped High Street, distant Helvellyn and the jutting Longstile Ridge between Blea Water and Haweswater

86

Route 19: Blea Water Crag Gill to High Street and Long Stile Ridge

	1	2	3
grade			*
quality			
navigation			

ASSESSMENT: Apart from the initial deep cleft, open and exposed scrambling follows the course of Blea Water Crag Gill and its overflow channels as they tumble for over 200m over slabby rocks, draining the summit of High Street.

GRADE NOTE: A serious scramble in an exposed situation, although the major difficulties are avoidable

OS MAP: Outdoor Leisure 5
GR: 469108
DISTANCE: 7km (4.5 miles) via High Street and Longstile Ridge

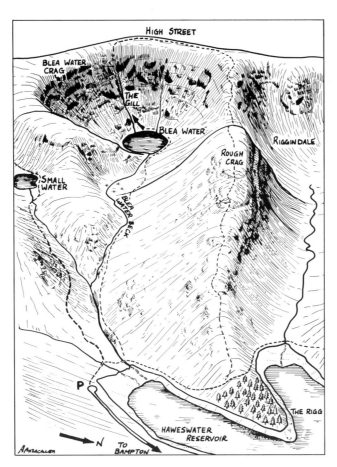

I like Haweswater, but I am sure I would have preferred it over 50 years ago before the village of Mardale Green disapeared under the rising waters of the reservoir. In recent dry summers the water level has dropped to expose the ghost of the old landscape and the bleached stones of its walls, drove roads and long-forgotten homes. For a while, before the rains came, it was possible to walk the cart tracks between the foundations of lost stone walls between farm buildings, the site of the ancient church and once busy Dun Bull Inn.

Mardale remains a backwater, perhaps because there are no villages or tea shops to attend to the tourist. The road simply ends at Mardale Head. If you find a lot of cars at the roadhead do not be dismayed; most will belong to 'twitchers' not scramblers. The Royal Society for the Protection of Birds has a particular interest in Riggindale and the rich birdlife on its crags. A pair of eagles nest here, and in recent years have managed to rear their young with the protection of the RSPB. The result is that birders flock here, oiled green and binocular clad, to 'ornithologise' and can be found lurking beneath rocks and bushes. Removed from mainstream lakeland life, the Eastern Fells have more than their fair share of wildlife: peregrine, buzzard and raven are a common sight, as are deer, badger and Charlie fox.

The semicircle of fells at the head of the dale offer a fine walk that takes in Harter Fell,

Mardale Ill Bell, High Street and Kidsty Pike. The scramble up Blea Water Crag Gill has become a regular outing of mine, since Mardale is less than 15 minutes from my door. As a route, it finds a bold and enjoyable line to the top of High Street, with the possibility of some open ridge walking to get back to Mardale Head.

From the car park at Mardale Head follow the footpath to the north side of Mardale Beck and climb steadily past waterfalls to the outfall of circular Blea Water, one of the deepest tarns, in the Lake District at 64m (210ft). On its far side a prominent gill cascades over slabs before plunging into a deep-cut cleft above scree. This is Blea Water Crag Gill. Traverse round the north side of the tarn to reach it (GR:446106).

The route climbs through steep terrain. In a freeze it provides good ice climbing, although it is usually an enjoyable and quite varied scramble, over 200m (650ft) long. After wet conditions it proves much more difficult as the rocks away from the gill are vegetative and slippery. The difficulties are not always avoidable, although with good route-finding and a bit of traversing easier ways can be found.

Climb directly up the deep cleft. It provides good sport and is best tackled on its right side away from the cascade. It is possible to exit on the left near the top. In spate it can be avoided by linking a series of terraces to the left of the watercourse. The rock in the gill bed is very good, quite smooth but washed clean and with reasonable friction.

After the initial step, terraces lead to a waterfall cascading over a step of black, lichened rock, above which is a clean water-washed slab. Follow the stream to the base of the waterfall, which can be avoided by a grassy ramp on the left. Alternatively, skirt the fall on the right, traversing left above it along an easy rake which is below the waterslide slab. This traverse allows you to gain an overflow channel on its left. An awkward step leads to easier ground. Great care is needed on this exposed section, particularly in wet, greasy conditions.

Follow the easiest line up the slabs before moving rightwards to make a hard move to reach a grassy ledge and easier ground. The main

Jane Pickvance scrambling high above sparkling Blea Water

watercourse is still to your right. Cross this by traversing horizontally to the far side of the gill. The difficulty and exposure now ease, with good clean rock leading upwards past a number of steps and waterfalls. The angle also relents considerably. On the right is a bristling rocky ridge of rough, clean rock. Climb along its delightful but all too short crest to gain grass slopes leading to the summit of High Street.

I can never tramp along High Street without recalling a marvellous poem of the same name by Tom Bowker, which recounts in ghostly form those who have walked and perished on the top since Roman times.

A blizzard caught me, on High Street.
Slamming the breath tight down my throat,
Flaying my face with ice.
Reeling, storm drunk, I fled for shelter.
Crouched shivering, by a black tarn,
My chilled hands jammed between my
   shivering thighs.

Although many think of the road over High Street as Roman, in fact as a route way it is much more ancient. Before the Romans trudged north to build their wall it was certainly a route used by Britons and later by the Celts.

To make a day of it you have several choices, all of which offer fine walking. The shortest and most dramatic route is down the narrow arm of Long Stile Ridge. This fine crest separates Riggindale and Blea Water Beck providing an exposed walk with magnificent views of the

Haweswater, Blea Water and the surrounding fells. If you are lucky you may even enjoy the spectacle of the eagles circling high above the hills or quartering the dark crags at the head of Riggindale.

There are alternatives but they are longer, although not by much. From High Street you can follow the path over gentle slopes to Mardale Ill Bell and descend to Nan Bield, the pass separating Kentmere and Mardale. If by then you have run out of steam you can descend a well made path past Small Water back to the car park. Alternatively, continue over craggy ground to the top of Harter Fell. From its summit the path then follows the boundary wall to Little Harter Fell and Adam

Barry White and Maurice McGlade on the final bristling ridge of rough clean rock

Seat before dropping to Gatescarth Pass where a gentle track that has been an important route way for centuries descends to Mardale Head.

The other fine walk from the top of this scramble goes northwards from High Street, following the track the legions took around the head of Riggindale towards High Raise. At the Head of Riggindale Beck you turn east towards Kidsty Pike to follow the path above the depths of Riggindale to Kidsty Howes, crossing the bridge over the beck at Bowderthwaite. Here a well trodden path, with a birdwatcher under every bush, leads back to Mardale Head.

Route 20: PINNACLE RIDGE, ST SUNDAY CRAG

	1	2	3
grade			
quality			
navigation			

ASSESSMENT: A fine ridge scramble, almost Alpine in style, that is all too short.
OS MAP: Outdoor Leisure 5

GR: 386169, Glenridding; 391163, Patterdale, limited parking
DISTANCE: 7km (4.5 miles) in a round from Patterdale

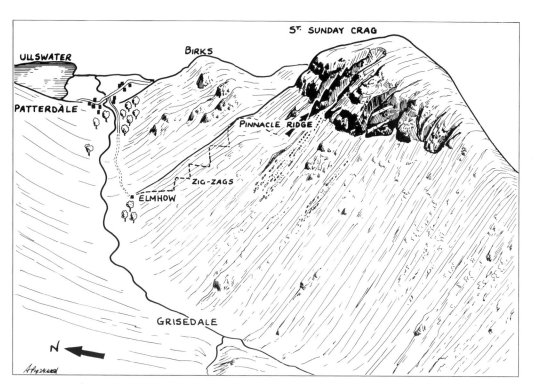

For those wanting a short day on one of the most enjoyable scrambles in the district, the ascent of Pinnacle Ridge on the Grisedale flank of St Sunday Crag has few comparisons. The name St Sunday is derived from St Dominic and the Latin *Dies Dominica,* the Lord's Day, which is wholly appropriate as that is when most of us are free to lift our eyes up, unto the hills.

A shortish day it might be but that is not to say it goes without effort. The walk up Grisedale is steady enough but the ease with which this is accomplished must be exchanged for the steep grind up the Elmhow zigzags, beginning by the south-west end of the Elmhow plantation. Care with route-finding is needed here as, low down, only a faint trod marks the route, although higher on the fell it becomes a good grass track. It is easy to begin the traverse towards the crag too early and end up crossing steep scree. Even if you find the right line, on a grassy shoulder close to the 500m (1640ft) contour the path leading to the foot of the crag still crosses some unstable ground.

Surprisingly the discovery of climbable crags on St Sunday is a relatively recent affair. Until the 1950s they had gone unnoticed. Pinnacle Ridge, now one of the most famous and most photographed scrambles in the Lakes, has the feel of a classic and pioneers such as the Abrahams or Hasket-Smith readily spring to mind. In fact, it was not until 1955 that G.A. Lever, Miss S.A. Evans, B.W. Lowthian and M.E.

Ben Holt descending to Patterdale from St Sunday Crag

Twentyman from the Sheffield University Mountaineering Club made the first ascent and the Pinnacle Ridge found its way into the guidebooks as a climb of moderate grade.

The face of St Sunday Crag is quite broken; the screes below are evidence of that. In fact, it is made up of a series of buttresses separated by deep-cut gullies. The path from Elmhow crosses quite low down below the crag, ending on scree beneath a gully right of Pinnacle Ridge. Climb up the scree to the foot of the ridge where a cairn on the edge of the gully marks the start. Although 'the Pinnacle' is hidden from below, a rowan can be seen on the right-hand side of the ridge 120m (394ft) or so above.

The scramble begins below this, up a ridge built of bristling blocks. It is quite narrow in places and is exposed where it overlooks the gully on the right. A slab, smooth in scrambling terms, can be avoided on the right by passing behind a block. This is followed by easy scrambling which leads to the base of the obvious Pinnacle with a distinctive smooth-cracked wall to its left. In the corner formed by the Pinnacle and the wall is easier ground, a groove; the crux of the route. Slow to dry out, the groove has bucket handholds and plenty of protection but can make you feel insecure if you get the sequence wrong. Once over this difficult step a rock arête leads a slab to the crest. Throughout this section there are good natural belays and spike runners for roped scrambling.

Ahead the crest of the ridge is 'airy' but good holds abound. An awkward move to overcome a slab, scratched by the crampons of winter climbers, lands you on a minor summit. These are the much photographed pinnacles and are best seen from the bilberry terraces ahead. From the last pinnacle descend a crest to a smooth, gently inclined slab and gain a col where the ridge butts against the summit slopes. These lead easily and quickly to the crest of St Sunday Crag. Although the major difficulties of this scramble are concentrated into less than 200m (656ft) of ridge the atmosphere of the ascent is altogether much grander, almost Alpine and well worth a visit, especially so on a sunny evening when that special lakeland light, perfectly captured by Heaton Cooper, floods Grisedale and the shadowy hollows of Nethermost, Ruthwaite and Cock Coves form a dramatic backdrop to the pinnacles. Only the isolated mirror of Hard Tarn below High Crags on Nethermost Pike glints from the shadows.

If your intention really is a short day on the hills, the path down the ridge to Patterdale is the fastest option. A slightly longer alternative route continues to Deepdale Hause where you have the choice of descending Deepdale or turning west to Grisedale Tarn and returning to Patterdale down Grisedale. The Grisedale Forest on the OS map does not exist on the ground as trees, and most probably dates from Norman times when the area was held under 'forest law' as a hunting reserve. In which case Grisedale, being the 'valley of pigs', might just refer to wild boar!

Bruce West enjoying an evening scramble on Pinnacle Ridge above Grisedale

Route 21: HELVELLYN'S HORSESHOE: STRIDING EDGE AND SWIRRAL EDGE

	1	2	3
grade			
quality			
navigation			

ASSESSMENT: The Lake District's classic ridge walk; open and exposed but no route-finding difficulties once on the ridge.

GRADE NOTE: Swirral Edge doesn't quite make grade 1 but with Striding Edge it makes a good day out

OS MAP: Outdoor Leisure 5
GR: 386170, ample car parking in Glenridding; and 391161, limited parking in Patterdale
DISTANCE: 9km (5.6 miles) via Catstye Cam

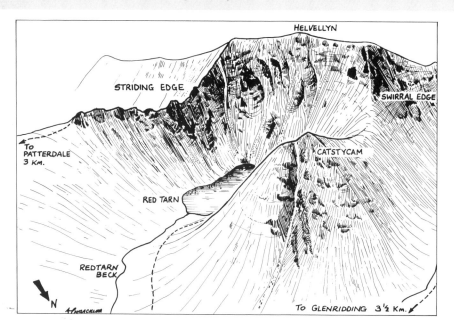

When summer's short lease has run its course and autumn's fine days are a memory, the scrambler needs to look carefully at what can be done in winter. I normally pray for snow and ice. Lovers of warm rock, on the other hand, who long for sunlit summits and babbling brooks, wait out the winter before returning to the ridges, gills and buttresses that are the natural habitat of the scrambler.

In order to enjoy the delights of winter, the scrambler must be prepared to learn new skills. Just as scrambling takes a giant's stride from walking towards rock climbing, winter scrambling involves another quantum leap in the level of skills, judgement, equipment and fitness needed. Even the easiest scramble can become a serious mountaineering challenge under a mantle of verglas and snow.

Take a walk around the Helvellyn Horseshoe, for instance. In summer both Striding and Swirral Edge are not too demanding; airy certainly, with steps that require the use of hands and feet and a head for heights. They represent the first level of scrambling on a continuum that leads to rock climbing. Under winter conditions, crusted in snow and ice, except for altitude they can be all but Alpine in character, calling for a mountaineer's craft with axe, rope and crampons. Even the easy bits – such as the slope to Helvellyn's summit from the end of Striding Edge, no more than a steep walk up a scree-covered path in summer – can seem like an

Eiger icefield under hard-packed snow and ice.

From my home in the Lakes I can see the hills and that can be a terrible torture when I am at my desk; they feel as remote as the mountains of the moon. After the first snows I am able to trace a sharp white line around Haweswater's skyline from my study window. Sometimes midweek, when the weather is perfect and the 'met-man' is forecasting a depression for the weekend, the temptation proves too much and I find myself heading for Helvellyn. Driving along Ullswater you can see the bulk of the mountain at the far end of the lake, deeply defined in monochrome, its sinuous ridges enhanced by snow.

Sallie O'Connor and Tim Naylor striding around Helvellyn's horseshoe

I usually park near Grisedale Bridge and tramp up the lane above Grisedale Beck. In summer or at weekends it can be hard to find a parking place although there is plenty in Glenridding. By the time you cross the bridge and begin the long pull to Grisedale Brow the tarmac is far behind you. Those not familiar with the Lakes and the conundrum of local names might be forgiven for being unable to find Patterdale Common on the steep hillside above Grisedale, if by 'common' you expect an acreage of flattish grazing land. Harder still to fathom is the slope of grass, bracken and ling below Eagle Crag, named Grisedale Forest on the OS map. Grisedale is a Norse name meaning 'Valley of the Pigs'. Perhaps pigs of yore, running short of truffles, went for the trees instead!

STRIDING EDGE

It does not take long to reach Grisedale Brow or the stile over the mountain wall giving access to Striding Edge. Helvellyn is a mountain mass that extends from Grisedale Hause in the south to Sticks Pass in the north. Along this length are the summits of Dollywagon Pike, Nethermost Pike, Helvellyn, Whiteside and Raise. Its eastern flank, sculptured by glaciation, is a series of cwms and coves (Keppel Cove, Brown Cove, Red Tarn and Nethermost Cove), separated by precipitous rocky ridges, the best of which are Striding and Swirril. Together they form the Helvellyn Horseshoe – the most popular ridge scramble in Cumbria, and rightly so.

Navigation is never a problem on Striding Edge; once over the wall the path leads straight to it. Before long it becomes rocky, soon narrowing down to the famous ice-hewn arrête. In good conditions you can walk along the crest, in places pavement wide. There is a path on the Red Tarn flank that avoids the best scrambling. In winter conditions, with a dusting of ice and snow, care and crampons are necessary. The ridge does rise and fall, but gently. The pleasure lies in walking a tight line along its crest and scrambling down the rocky steps into a notch and then out again to stride along a natural pavement of smooth blocks. For a lover of exposed places the name of this ridge more than lives up to it. An awkward descent down a steep groove provides the crux at the end of the ridge.

Throughout the Lake District you can see layers of history exposed like folded strata on a quarry face. Each layer reveals the links between man and the land since early times. The Celts, or Cymry, who give their name to Cumbria itself, the Romans, Angles, Saxons, Irish and Norsemen are all represented. The name of every hill, dale, lake and gill reflects their passing. Nor only ancient events have left their mark on Striding Edge; along the route there is a plaque to a fallen huntsman and a monument to a fallen poet and his trusty hound, all part of Helvellyn's saga.

I remember a moment of *déjà vu* while scrambling on Striding Edge. Just after passing the plaque to the huntsman a bright-eyed mutt scurried past me. Almost unseen it brushed my leg and continued searching along the ridge. At that moment it was as if the spectre of Charles Gough's dog was haunting the place and, for a brief moment, the hairs on the back of my neck lifted. Gough was a poet who died from a fall from Striding Edge on 18 April 1805. For 3 months his bitch, a yellow rough-haired terrier, stayed with his body until they were discovered on 20 July.

Only just alive and terribly emaciated the dog had kept watch over her master's body and her own newly born pups, found dead. Sadly the bitch died soon after being found. Today all are remembered in a monument close to the summit and in poems by William Wordsworth and Walter Scott. Thankfully my ghostly apparition soon reappeared with its master – alive and real.

SWIRRAL EDGE

To gain the top of Swirral Edge skirt the top of the Red Tarn face of Helvellyn to where a cairn marks the start of a rocky path descending steeply down this shorter, less dramatic edge. For the best scrambling you need to stay on the arrête, although an easier walker's path crisscrosses the ridge. Rather than leave the edge to traverse round the tarn to regain Grisedale Brow, stay with the ridge and walk to the top of Catstye Cam – a strange name which is a mixture of Norse and Old English meaning 'a steep wild cat's path'. It is then easy enough to descend to Glenridding or return to the Brow and Patterdale.

SOUTH-WESTERN FELLS

Route 22: Low-level scrambles around Wasdale: Pike Crag, Iron Crag, Nether Beck Gorge, Bowderdale Boulder and Bell Rib

	1	2	3
grade (Pike Crag)			
grade (Iron Crag)		*	
grade (Nether Beck Gorge)			
grade (Bell Rib)		*	
quality			
navigation			

ASSESSMENT: A varied selection of low-level scrambles suitable for a short day or when the higher fells are out of condition. There are plenty of options at all grades.

GRADE NOTE: Bowderdale Boulder can be as easy or as difficult as you care to make it
OS MAP: Outdoor Leisure 6
GR: 136055, Buckbarrow; 162066, Nether Beck Bridge; or 108068, Overbeck Bridge
DISTANCE: All are close to the road. It is up to you to discover a logical way of linking them

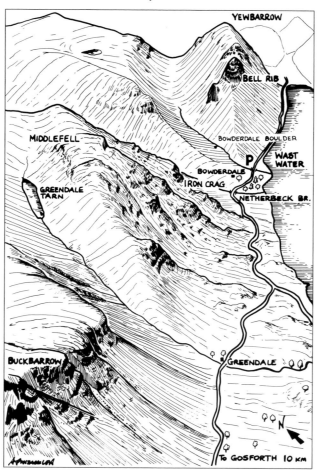

It is little wonder that Wasdale became the cradle of Lake District climbing. With its many crags and the Lake District's highest mountains, it must have seemed a paradise to Haskett-Smith, Owen Glynn Jones, the Abrahams and the other pioneers on Cumbrian rock. Not only that, it had the other essential ingredient: a comfortable inn. Today things are much the same. If you want to climb on the finest crag in England, Wasdale Head with its now famous hotel is the natural base for walking, climbing or scrambling. There is good camping, a well stocked equipment shop just in case you've forgotten something, and thankfully little else, making it an almost perfect base from which to enjoy the hills.

Whereas it is possible to see how rock climbing evolved from the gill and gully era to broken buttresses and onto the blank sweep of steep faces, scrambling seeks no such progression of difficulty but remains with many of the climbs that were the foundation stones of British rock climbing. They were pioneered in the days when a 'leader did not fall' – more than once that is! This is an adage that should certainly hold true for the unroped scrambler.

To the pioneers the real interest lay with the higher crags and gullies on mountains like Pillar, Gable, Great End and, of course, Scafell. One of the good things about many scrambles is that they can be climbed in most conditions, although it takes a 'special' sort of person to venture up a thundering watercourse on a cold day or find much delight in lichened, loose rock on a wet and windy one. However, there are routes to be had whatever the weather or time of year. Of course, personal skill and tolerance of discomfort are often essential for success and even then, in rotten conditions, I have witnessed 'extreme' leaders wobble and retreat from an out-of-condition scramble.

Although Wasdale is better known for its 'giants' – the Scafells, Gable, Great End, Red Pike and Pillar – it also has some delightful 'lower fells' that have a surprising amount of good, clean rock, set at just the right angle for an enterprising scrambler. As you drive up Wasdale your eyes are naturally drawn to the famous fells surrounding Wasdale Head but long before you reach them there is a trilogy of smaller peaks well worth exploring. One of them, Yewbarrow, will naturally catch your attention. Looking like an upturned Viking longship, its keel-like main ridge leads your eye into the Mosedale Horseshoe. There is plenty of scrambling to be found on its rocky outcrops.

On the way to Yewbarrow you have to pass two other fells, Buckbarrow and Middle Fell. Both have an abundance of open rock and there is at least one unusual gorge scramble along Nether Beck. Should you find yourself wanting a shorter day, or if the higher routes are out of condition, take time to explore these

Bill O'Connor on the final fall in Lower Nether Beck Gorge

gems: you will be well rewarded and pleasantly surprised!

PIKE CRAG – BUCKBARROW GR:136057

The first of the scrambles is at Buckbarrow where there have been some recent rock climbing developments although, back in the 1890s, Norman Collie, of Skye fame, was the first to establish routes here. Buckbarrow is really the rocky toe of a larger, rounded fell, Seatallan, and is the interesting craggy terrain contained between Greendale Gill and Gill Beck. This assortment of crags and buttresses separated by deep gullies faces south, and so comes into condition quite quickly.

The road between Gosforth and Wasdale via Greendale passes close under Buckbarrow, with parking possible where the road comes closest to the crags. This scramble takes the rough, sound rock of Pike Crag on its right-hand side where a scree-filled gully defines a rock ridge on the edge of the crag. This corresponds very closely with Left Face Climb, first done by Collie, King and Brunskill in April 1892. Reach the base of the scramble by first ascending close to the dry stone wall under Long Crag and then traversing rightwards under crags to the foot of the scramble, where a tree marks the start of the route.

The upper section of the scramble follows the well defined rock ridge but to reach it the lower buttress, left of the ridge, has to be dealt with. An intricate and interesting scramble overcomes this first difficulty at a surprisingly easy level – as long as the right route is followed!

Start just right of the holly and ascend easily rightwards towards a cleft in the edge of the cliff. A heathery ledge below this cleft leads back left to a secondary rib. Move left across this to another ledge marked by precarious blocks before ascending rightwards to avoid a vegetative slab, and so reach the base of a steep wall. Traverse to the right beneath this wall to an easy rake which can be followed to another poised block. Pass behind this block, moving leftwards, and scramble up a rock rib which leads to the edge of the buttress overlooking the scree-filled gully.

The main difficulties are now behind you. Ahead is the rocky arête which can be followed to the top, avoiding any difficulties on the left until the scrambling eases and the Buckbarrow's cairn is reached.

IRON CRAG – MIDDLE FELL GR:156066

Middle Fell is not far from the first scramble and is a delightful and complicated mass contained between Greendale Gill and Nether Beck which offers a fair amount of exposed rock. It provides an ideal playground for an evening's scrambling, when trying to link one outcrop with another makes for a most interesting and continuous route to the top. The best and longest routes can be found linking the rocks of Iron Crag overlooking Bowderdale. This is ideally approached by a direct ascent from Netherbeck Bridge where the lowest rocks of the crag can be seen bounding the right side of a wide gully, vegetative and scree-filled, with a large single yew tree in the middle of its bed. There are plenty of scrambling options up this buttress which slopes up rightwards and, in fact, it is made up of four separate tiers. The most difficult way finds a direct route on the left side of the rocks close to the edge of the gully. By moving right the difficulties can be eased.

When the scrambling runs out, another band of slabs leading to the summit can be seen over on the left, a short walk away. Once again you have a variety of options; the easiest line is up the right-hand side of these slabs. In turn, this connects with rocky steps that lead all the way to the summit.

NETHER BECK GORGE GR:161071

Just beyond Nether Beck Bridge on the Wasdale Road, a footpath runs north alongside the beck towards Haycock. Although passing close to the stream, its two narrow, deep-cut gorges remain hidden beneath a canopy of trees. Both deserve closer inspection because they offer interesting sport, particularly on a hot day when the ennui of the hills can overcome even the most enthusiastic scrambler. However, if you want to complete a round of all the scrambles in this chapter, you would do well to leave this one till last. Your chances of returning dry shod, or even dry clothed, from Nether Beck's gorges are remote – this is no wadi and success will inevitably depend on wading pools to connect dry rock; an interesting and unusual experience.

From the bridge walk upstream until you reach the first section of gorge. A pool needs to be passed on the left to reach a waterfall, which is also passed by starting on the left. At this point the gorge is already quite deep with a profusion of trees, bushes, ferns and flowers, altogether a delightful place that fills with sunshine filtered through curtains of green on a good day. Continue over boulders above the fall into the narrowing gorge where more pools offer aquatic interest, until a larger cascade provides the finale to the initial ravine. Once again, the left side offers the line of least resistance. A series of bold steps onto flat ledges leads to an exit where a tree provides a final handhold.

The second gorge can be reached by walking upstream to where a rocky cleft begins, downstream from where Black Beck joins the main stream below Rough Crag. On the way to it you pass by numerous beautiful cascades. One in particular, the meeting of four overflow channels with a deep plunge pool beneath, is a family favourite for summer bathing. The rock wall on the right offers a small challenge but not as great as the deep and welcoming water below.

For the second section follow the bouldery stream bed into the steep-sided gorge, making progress by wading pools and crossing boulders to go deeper into its increasingly steep-sided and verdant bowels. A small fall can be passed but this leads immediately to a deep pool that is best passed on the left. Success here is not about staying dry but about how much of you gets wet. Long legs are an advantage. Beyond this obstacle another fall is best passed on the right before a rock provides an underwater stepping stone, letting you bypass a big boulder. Beyond this more boulders and pools provide unusual interest all the way to the end of the gorge.

BOWDERDALE BOULDER GR:166077

Since many scrambles were first explored by the pioneers of lakeland climbing, it would be a pity to overlook this low level landmark on a day when the tops hold little attraction. It is found beside the beck below Dropping Crag and provides a variety of problems and all manner of difficulty and steepness. The most ancient routes are at its upstream end whilst the steep lines are to the south. Those looking for the positively overhanging should try climbing from the table of rock nearest the stream.

BELL RIB – YEWBARROW GR: 170075

From Overbeck Bridge on the Wasdale Road a footpath runs alongside a wall running up the keel-like ridge of Yewbarrow to below an attractive cone of rock – Bell Rib. Several climbs in the moderate – difficult category were established here in 1927 and it is the scene for the final scramble in this low-level selection. From the top of the dry stone wall, ascend steeply over broken ground to the foot of the rocks. Left of these and slightly higher is a large boulder. Gain this and climb a groove until it merges into the crag and easier scrambling leads steeply to the top of the crag. By continuing over Bell Rib you enter Great Door, the deep-cut cleft that follows a rock fault, the passage through which leads to Bull Crag and eventually to the top of Yewbarrow.

Easier scrambling in the middle section of Netherbeck Gorge

101

Route 23: SOUTH-EAST FACE OF ILL CRAG, ESKDALE
AND THE HIGHEST SUMMIT IN ENGLAND

	1	2	3
grade			
quality			
navigation			

ASSESSMENT: One of the longest continuous scrambles in the Lake District with an enjoyable but fairly long approach. Open slab scrambling with plenty of route options.

GRADE NOTE: Difficulties can be avoided to give grade 1 and 2 variations
OS MAPS: Outdoor Leisure 6 and slight overlap with 4
GR: 235123
DISTANCE: 13.5km (8.4 miles) with a lot of ascent and descent

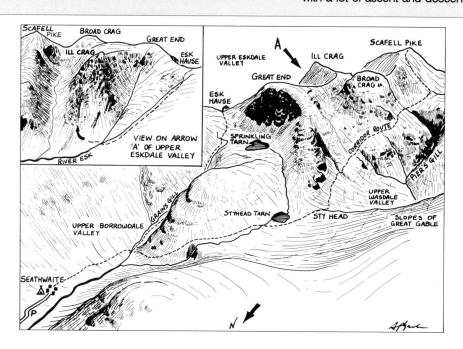

By lakeland standards upper Eskdale is a remote and wild place, a haven of rough rock and quiet solitude. It forms a natural corridor through the heart of the highest peaks of the district and not surprisingly has been a routeway since ancient times. The flanks of the Esk above the Great Moss are girdled by the rocky buttresses of Scafell, Scafell Pike, Ill Crag and Esk Pike. It is truly a scrambler's paradise, with some of the longest buttress routes in the Lakes and well worth the effort to get there.

From the south there are approaches on either side of the Hardknott Pass, either from Cockley Beck and Mosedale or Brotherilkeld along the Esk River itself. To lighten this long approach the Esk sports a fine gorge between Lingcove Bridge and Great Moss which provides one of the finest scrambles of its kind in the Lakes. Even when climbed in dry conditions on a hot day, there is no guarantee that you will stay dry for long! Above the Great Moss continue to Little Narrowcove, a tributary of the Esk, following the route to Mickledore where a path returns to the Great Moss, or continue to Scafell and descend via Long Green and Slight Side, south to Brotherilkeld on the river Esk.

Based in the Northern Lakes, I normally approach Eskdale from Borrowdale, opting to cross Esk Hause and descend into the upper valley. The route described offers a superb scramble, the south east face of Ill Crag, Scafell

Pike, the highest summit in England, and a return via the Corridor Route to Styhead Tarn and Seathwaite; all in all, a great day out.

From the farm at Seathwaite, which has been farmed by Stan Edmondson for more than 60 years and, in fact, by his family for more than 150, follow the path south up Grains Gill. If it should be raining at Seathwaite do not be surprised; records show it to be the wettest inhabited place in England with over 300cm (120in) of rain a year! Higher up the track Ruddy Gill provides a scrambler's alternative to the path and leads all the way to below Great End. On the path, rough walking then leads quickly to Esk Hause, the pass between Esk Pike and Great End. Cross this and descend into upper Eskdale passing through the narrow gorge of the Knotts of the Tongue, keeping to the true right bank of the river. Before Skilling Crag contour the hillside to gain Little Narrowcove and the base of the south-east face of Ill Crag (GR:226068); a broken, rocky hillside providing continuous open scrambling to the top with a vertical interval of almost 500m (1640ft). Eric Shipton, instructing with Eskdale Outward Bound, often took students on this route. *The Times* journalist Ronnie Faux was one of them and he first introduced me to this fine scramble.

As you look up Little Narrowcove, aim to climb the lowest slabs on the right of the stream just left of a mossy rock wall. The initial slab leads to a ledge and a steeper slab which is best climbed by a groove on the left. Above, easy slabs lead to a grassy bay, which is crossed to reach a bilberry ramp leading to a rock step. Climb this to gain a rock rib on the left which takes you below a block-capped rock wall. Scramble up right to gain a heathery hollow. Now follow a groove on the right which leads to a rake, left of the crest, and so gain a mossy slab. Continue up slabs right of the crest to reach a grassy break below a steep central wall, well seen from below.

Above is an impressive sweep of slabs made for climbing. A vegetative groove on the left provides the only feasible route for scrambling and even then the use of a rope is advised. Gain the

Chris Brasher in the middle of the crux slabs on Ill Crag

groove from the slabs on the right and follow this until a flake at the top gives access to the rock rib on the left. Move back right and climb the rock rib and a steep step to reach scree and easy ground.

Above lies the third step. Go diagonally left towards a deep vegetative gully with a rock nose below and to the right. Do not climb the gully but gain a pedestal on the right. Traverse the nose and gain easy ground up to the right. Move left to a buttress with a groove to the right of a well defined edge. Climb the groove and gain the exposed left edge with difficulty. This is bordering on rock climbing but can be outflanked on the right. Above, a grass ramp leads to a well defined and delightful rock rib, the final step. Follow it to the summit of Ill Crag.

For a speedy return, follow the footpath north-east towards Great End, descending Calf Cove to Esk Hause and return to Seathwaite. My proposal, however, is to hop the boulders to Broad Crag and continue to the jewel in England's crown, Scafell Pike.

From the summit there are plenty of options. Either follow the path north-west, over rough ground, towards Lingmell Col to cross Piers Gill at the fords and gain the Corridor Route to Sty Head. Alternatively, a longer more difficult option is to descend to Mickledore and ascend Scafell by Broad Stand (Grade 3, p20).

The first recorded descent of this was made by the poet Samuel Taylor Coleridge in 1802. The fact that he and countless others have had an epic climb on this difficult step suggests it should not be treated lightly. The crux is a smooth corner above an exposed sloping ledge. Holds on the left wall hold the key but are less than substantial in wet conditions.

From the summit either return to Mickledore via Broad Stand or descend Lord's Rake to traverse under the cliffs of Pikes Crag, and then to Lingmell Col, and so gain the Corridor Route. From Styhead Tarn follow the footpath to Taylorgill Force, keeping to the true left bank of the river. The path traverses the flank of Base Brown to Sourmilk Gill and Seathwaite.

Glen Andrew climbing the rock rib right of the bilberry ramp

Route 24: ILL GILL, KIRK FELL AND THE MOSEDALE SKYLINE WITH NETHER BECK GORGE

	1	2	3
grade (Ill Gill)			*
grade (Nether Beck Gorge)			
quality			
navigation			

ASSESSMENT: A long and difficult gill scramble, if taken direct, in a superb situation; followed by one of the finest ridge walks in the Lakes and an optional, refreshing descent to finish the day.

GR: 186088, Wasdale Head
OS MAP: Outdoor Leisure 6 and slight overlap with 4
DISTANCE: 15km (9.4 miles) via Yewbarrow; 10km (6.2 miles) via Wind Gap and Mosedale

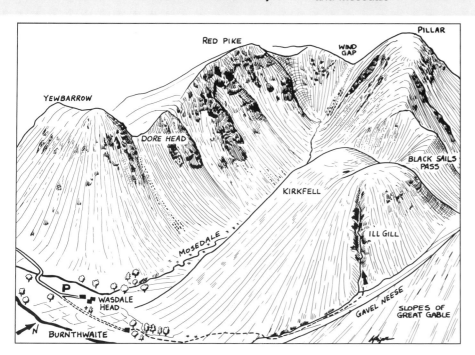

There are lots of ills in the Lake District; and when I say that I am not dropping me aitches, meaning big ills and little ills. What I have in mind are those steep, deep, running-with-water ills of the 'gill and crag' variety. As Robert Gambles points out in his marvellous little book, *Lake District Place Names*, the commonly used prefix 'ill' comes from the Old Norse 'illr' meaning steep or precipitous. So just as the Alps has a multitude of Mont Blancs, the Lake District is steeped in ills.

Wasdale, as you would expect, has its fair share of ill places. As you drive down Wast Water Lake its famous screes plummet over 500m (1640ft) from aptly named Illgill Head to the water. To the north of Wasdale Head, broad-summited Kirk Fell presents a gentle flank, concealing its more interesting places from the casual observer.

ILL GILL

To get to grips with Kirk Fell's Ill Gill you must first climb the flank of Gavel Neese to a point where it joins Gable Beck. No watercourse is better named. The Gill drops from Illgill Head, fed by Kirkfell Tarn which, in fact, comprises two small, shallow tarns nestling in a hollow between the twin summits of the mountain. In all, there is a drop of over 370m (1214ft), with three major difficulties that should only be attempted in dry conditions. However, all are avoidable, in which case the gill is a grade easier.

This provides a superb scramble, difficult if climbed direct, and a good way to start a round of the Mosedale Horseshoe.

Enter the gill bed direct and enjoy a scramble past deep pools to the base of the first big fall. Pass this on the right and continue without difficulty to a smaller, interesting cascade leading to an obvious exit from the gill on the right. The rock so far is good and in dry conditions provides good friction. In spring and early summer, the walls of this steep-sided gorge are lined with flowers, in particular primrose and anemone. Take care with the trees as their roothold is precarious and many end up slipping into the stream bed.

The next section of the gill holds some difficult falls which are not scrambling terrain. Also, the rock above changes to andesite which is shattered and friable; so beware, as many of the holds simply break off. After a difficult move to bridge past a small fall the gorge ahead narrows and you will see two high falls. By all means have a look at them but do not attempt them as scrambling. Instead, you can leave the gill on the right where a trod leads past a tree to the edge of the gorge and the steep hillside.

Re-enter above the main fall at a point where a scree shoot and a grassy hollow give access to the stream bed. The gill above now cascades down a series of steps, offering good scrambling mainly on the left of the stream. As ever, the

Classic gill scrambling on superb rock in Ill Gill

state of the water will dictate the line. Just after you regain the gill a fall of perhaps 8m (26ft) offers a delightful pitch up a slab to the left of the water. The holds are superb and the rock pale and solid. Above this a larger fall is best climbed on the left up crumbly, vegetative rock. This difficult pitch leads to a small amphitheatre with an exit up to the right to avoid a difficult direct ascent of the gill bed.

The atmosphere of Ill Gill is superb, the best that gill scrambling has to offer. Having avoided the difficulty, return to the gill for more sport as it is now more broken. Stay with the main bed of the gill and continue to the tarns or the western summit. The views from the rounded bulk of Kirk Fell are superb: Great Gable, Great End, the Scafells and the whole of the Mosedale Horseshoe are on display.

From the summit the next leg of the round is a descent north-west to Black Sail Pass by way of Kirkfell Crags. Once at the pass the long pull to Pillar beckons. If you are out for a full scrambling day Pillar Rock is not a great detour, and Slab and Notch or the Old West Route are classics of their class.

Failing that, continue over Pillar and descend south-west to Wind Gap. Then make the stiff pull to Little Scoat Fell, being sure to traverse out to Steeple, the rocky, projecting ridge that gives the fell its meaning. The panorama from Steeple to Pillar and distant Kirk Fell is impressive. It continues in a sweep over dark Ennerdale towards Haycock which dominates the view across Mirkiln Cove.

NETHER BECK GORGE

To complete the round you must turn your back on dark tree'd Ennerdale and retrace your steps for a while to regain the long arm of the ridge leading to Red Pike, traversing high above the deep pool of Scoat Tarn. At almost 615m (2018ft) above sea level it is one of the highest in Cumbria. If you are lucky enough to be out in hot weather after a dry spell, you may be tempted to leave the ridge after Red Pike and descend to Scoat Tarn to explore the gorges of Netherbeck. Hidden from the nearby path, the narrow cleft is in places over 30m (98ft) deep, made secret and mysterious by a canopy of trees. A descent of the gorges is particularly worthwhile, especially in hot weather after a tiring day, and since it is almost impossible to avoid wet feet and thighs, why not go in for a swim? What better way is there to refresh yourself before the inevitable road walk back to Wasdale Head?

Should you forgo the pleasure, stay on the skyline ridge over Red Pike to Dore Head with its tiny unnamed tarn. From here there are two logical possibilities: either descend very steeply down worn-out Dorehead Screes to Mosedale, or continue over Stirrup Crag to Yewbarrow and descend via Bull Crag and Great Door to the road near Overbeck Bridge and the hike along the road to Wasdale Head.

Approaching Ill Gill with Lingmell and Broad Crag beyond

Route 25: GABLE: NAPES NEEDLE, EAGLE'S NEST GULLY, ARROWHEAD RIDGE AND WESTMORLAND CRAG

	1	2	3
grade (Napes Needle)			
grade (Eagle's Nest Gully)	*		
grade (Arrowhead Ridge)			
grade (Westmorland Crag)			
quality			
navigation			

ASSESSMENT: A classic route amongst the best mountain scenery in the Lakes. A fine contrast between an enclosed gully, an open ridge and a buttress close to the summit.

GR: 186088, Wasdale Head; 235122, Seathwaite
OS MAP: OS Outdoor Leisure 6 (from Wasdale) or 4 (from Seathwaite)
DISTANCE: 11km (6.9 miles) via Kirk Fell and Black Sail Pass

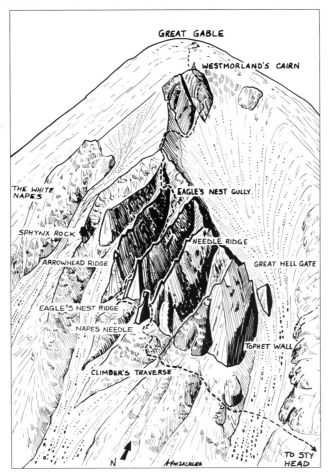

More than any valley in the Lakes Wasdale, and in particular the hotel at Wasdale Head, is the traditional home of mountaineers. Throughout Britain there are places, hotels and pubs that have become the natural focus for climbers once off the hill. The P-y-G in North Wales, the Sligachan on Skye, the Clachaig in Glen Coe and, of course, the Old Dungeon Ghyll in Langdale. As a breed, mountaineers may be famed for their independence and introversion, but I believe they delight in company and swapping yarns and there's no better place for that than Wasdale Head. No activity provides greater contrasts than mountaineering, where a day on the lonely fells can be followed by an evening reliving the day's epics around a warm fire in good company.

The first time I visited Wasdale it felt very remote. It was in winter and we crossed on foot from Langdale which was quicker than making the long drive around the southern end of the Lakes. From the Honister or Seathwaite in Borrowdale the approach is even shorter. Today, with better roads and faster cars, it seems no less remote. Negotiating the narrow lanes through Santon Bridge and Nether Wasdale feels like a journey into the past, but it is a journey well worth making. The Wasdale Head, a fine old hotel, remains the natural focus and good camping nearby provides an ideal base from which to explore the finest mountains in England.

Surrounding Wasdale Head are a full hand of high fells: Red Pike, Kirk Fell, Great Gable, Great End, Broad Crag, Scafell Pike and Scafell. Somehow it is Gable that looks the most attractive, perhaps because it seems more isolated between deep-cut Gable and Lingmell Beck. It rises steeply beyond a crossword puzzle of walled fields where the smooth angle of Gavel Neese gives way to scree and a barrier of angular crags whose dark rocks conceal Napes Needle and some superb scrambling.

NAPES NEEDLE

Napes Needle is a natural monument to our sport. First climbed in 1886 by Walter Parry Haskett-Smith, its ascent marks the beginning in Britain of rock climbing as a sport rather than as a training excuse for higher, greater things. Originally known as the Gable Needle, Owen Glynn Jones in his guide to *Rock Climbs in the English Lake District* points out that Wilson Robinson had made a pencil drawing of it in 1828. The route to its top, daringly soloed by Haskett-Smith, is well beyond scrambling but since it acts as a marker to better things it is only right and proper to make a pilgrimage to it and around it. The first problem for those not familiar with Napes Crag is to find the Needle. In poor visibility this is not as easy as it might seem because the pinnacle, although isolated, is not huge and readily merges with the crag behind and above it.

A view of the needle from the Dress Circle

From Wasdale Head a path leads between walls to Burnthwaite where, after crossing Gable Beck, it picks up another altogether steeper path that ascends the broad ridge of Gavel Neese, towards White Napes. Although you can climb directly up Gavel Neese, a more interesting and less tiring approach is to follow Moses Trod, the well made sledgate that leads to the Honister mines. At first glance it might seem that the track went directly up Gavel Neese, but in fact it was graded for horses pulling heavy sleds loaded with slate, and sometimes illicit brandy and Seathwaite wadd. Sensibly it climbs more slowly from Wasdale Head to Sty Head, from where it crosses Great Gable below Kern Knotts, traversing the scree-covered hillside below Great and White Napes. This approach provides a much more inter-esting route to the crags and opens up the whole box of delights that Gable has to offer.

Soon after leaving Sty Head the great walls and cracks of Kern Knotts rises above the path. Anyone with an interest in Lake District climbing would have seen pictures and postcards of its famous 'sentry box' crack. Huge boulders, remnants of a collapse that formed Kern Knotts' geometry, litter the path. Thread your way through or over these and rise diagonally on a path that crosses towards Napes Crag. A short way beyond Napes the path passes close to a small rock cave well worth knowing about, as it provides the last drinking water on the long dry pull to the summit of Gable. The next obvious feature will be found underfoot in the form of red rock fragments that make up the scree of Great Hell Gate. Once crossed it leads under the impressive rock face of Tophet Wall; a Gable classic. Further on, the path crosses steeper ground much closer to the flying buttress of rock that form Napes Ridges. At a point where the path divides take the upper fork. It leads steeply up, either in a vague gully or on pleasant rock steps, to the right of the base of Napes Needle.

Since we are on a pilgrimage and Napes is all but sacred to mountaineers (although blasphemers once planned to blow it up), our journey would not be complete without 'Threading the Needle.' Unlike the Sherpas who walk clockwise around their sacred *mani* walls, our scrambling takes us in the other direction. Go steeply up to the base of a groove behind the Needle and climb, edge or scramble up this to the notch separating the Needle from the main crag. Beyond is a climber's heaven, a kingdom of rock and steep ridges, but first you must pass through the eye of the needle – not as easy as it looks.

Looking across from the notch at roughly the same level, you should be able to make out Sphinx Rock. Descend to and cross the gully beyond to rock ledges known as the Dress Circle, the traditional spot from which to watch

Pulling out of Eagle's Nest Gully with the deep trench of Wasdale below

and photograph climbers on the Needle. If you look back to the Needle a wide crack splits the face in a left-to-right diagonal leading to a balcony below the final point; in fact a balanced block. Haskett-Smith's solo took him up the crack to the balcony and then by way of an exposed and bold mantleshelf to the very point of the Needle.

EAGLE'S NEST GULLY

Continue across ledges below Eagle's Nest Ridge and go through a 'crevasse' behind an obvious rock flake to reach Eagle's Nest Gully, left of which is Arrowhead Ridge. Begin by climbing up the left side of the gully before a vegetative crack leads left, followed by a diagonal crack leading rightwards. This is quite exposed and not altogether solid but lets you gain the bed of the gully above a chockstone.

The view into Wasdale from this point is very impressive and the Arrowhead rock flake is an impressive feature on the right. All this is amongst awesome scenery, but beware underfoot of the loose rock and scree, taking care not to knock any on others traversing below the crag. Where the gully divides the central line is the one to take. The rock here can be very greasy, even after a dry spell. Take care to follow the line of least resistance up the gully which bends leftwards to a grassy ramp, which lands you on the crest of Arrowhead Ridge.

ARROWHEAD RIDGE AND WESTMORLAND CRAG

Continue up the crest staying with the ridge, climbing an obvious crack to reach some blocks. Slabs and more broken ground then lead to a grassy spur that connects with another rock rib which can be followed to the top of Napes Crag.

The main path to the summit can be joined here. It avoids Westmorland Crag by a detour to the left. A scrambling route climbs the crag direct to Westmorland cairn. Traverse right beneath the crag to a square-capped block. Climb the spur above this, followed by a series of rock steps. Avoid the obvious gully to the right by going left to reach another spur behind a gendarme and continue up the crest on interesting rock to the top of the crag.

It is a short walk to the summit of Great Gable from the cairn, with plenty of options for a return to Wasdale. Traversing the mountain north-east to Windy Gap and taking in Green Gable is one. Alternatively, descend from the Gap into Stone Cove or, better still, stay on the higher path that traverses under Gable Crag and descends to Beck Head. From here you can pick up Moses Trod to Wasdale. If your legs are up to it, traversing Kirk Fell and descending by way of Black Sail Pass and Gatherstone Beck is my preferred option.

Pulling on jugs up the final step of Arrowhead Ridge – much easier than it looks

Route 26: Esk Gorge and Cam Spout to Mickledore and Scafell

	1	2	3
grade (Sourmilk Gill)		*	
grade (Rabbit's Trod)		*	
quality			
navigation			

ASSESSMENT: A scramble up the loveliest mountain stream in Cumbria followed by steeper climbing up Cam Spout and the logical option of Broad Stand to Scafell's summit.

GR: 212012, Brotherilkeld; 24016, Cockley Beck Bridge
OS MAP: Outdoor Leisure 6
DISTANCE: 15.5km (9.7 miles) via Stony Tarn

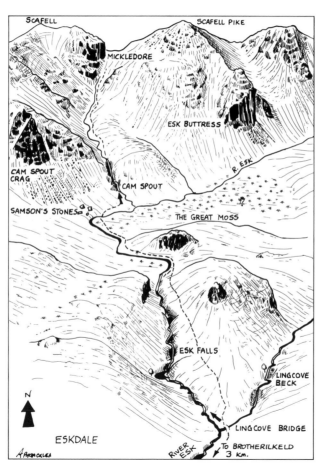

Climbing Scafell always provides a long, hard mountain day, especially when your approach is from the south along the River Esk and Great Moss. The river begins its southward journey on the grassy slopes below Esk Hause, between Great End and Esk Pike. It gathers force rapidly to cut through a narrow ravine called the Knotts of the Tongue as it tumbles down a rocky course to a meeting with the beck from Little Narrowcove. Shortly beyond this confluence the valley widens and flattens, absorbing the stream in the sponge of the Great Moss. The Great Moss seems once to have been a lake bed retained behind the barrier of rock known as Scar Lathing. Beyond the Scar the river has once again been forced to cut its course, narrowing between Throstlehow and Green Crag to form a delightful gorge. Tackled in drier conditions, the gorge of the Esk is a wonderful scramble on sound, rough rock amongst delightful scenery. On a hot summer's day you will be hard pressed to stay out the of the deep pools that compete for perfection amongst serious skinny dippers. Below the gorge the Esk is swollen by Lingcove Beck which is spanned by a packhorse bridge.

A good friend and climbing partner, Ronnie Faux, first recommended the Esk Gorge to me as an alternative scrambling approach to the

View across the Great Moss to Scafell Pike and the start of Cam Spout

remote delights on Esk Buttress. In my haste to get to the upper Esk I had walked past the pools, many hidden from the normal path, and had missed some of the hidden treasures of the Lake District.

You have a choice of two approaches. The path alongside the river from Brotherilkeld seems the most obvious and can be followed to Lingcove Bridge and the start of the gorge. An alternative approach from Cockley Beck Bridge further east is shorter but limits the return leg of the round if you want to avoid the same ground. On the other hand, if you want a longer day it is an ideal starting point for a round of the Scafells, Great End, Esk Pike, Bow Fell and Crinkle Crags. There is good campsite at Fisher Ground and plenty of hotel and farm-house accommodation in the valley. I particularly like Boot and friendly Brook House Hotel.

Esk Gorge

In scrambling up Esk Gorge you have to be prepared to get wet. Because the sidewalls are smooth, the only way many of the pools can be passed is by wading. Thus it seems sensible to wait for the right conditions and enjoy the warmth and water to the full.

After crossing the Cockley Beck Bridge pass a deep pool on the right to reach the first fall which should also be negotiated on the right. Easier ground then leads upstream to a

At the top of Greencove Wyke with Long Green behind

deepening, mossy trench. Cross the stream and pass the next pool and the waterfall above on the left. Recross the stream, passing the next large pool and cascade tumbling 12m (40ft) on the right. Stay on the same side to pass the next pool and before you regain the rocky stream bed. Cross to the left and then back right, passing one pool and wading the next, to enter the deepening gorge above yet another deep plunge pool.

The gorge ahead contains many inviting holes, whilst the name of the game is to stay out of them for as long as possible. This is easier said than done on a hot day or with damp rocks! Ahead you must enter the green ravine and pass the next fall and its deep pool on the right. Go left and then back right past another pool before traversing the steep left wall past two more pools. Now make a short descent and a tricky traverse which leads to a huge rock-blocking progress up the ravine. Climb around this by a steep crack which gives access to a final improbable pool, which can be avoided or passed, with difficulty, on the right.

CAM SPOUT

The Great Moss is above and beyond, providing views of the wild fells of the upper Esk and the finest flank of Scafell. You can either cross the Moss or traverse to Sampson's Stones before making your way to the foot of Cam Spout, the final triumphant plunge of How Beck before it soaks into the Great Moss.

The route towards Mickledore climbs up right of the fall. Taken direct, Cam Spout provides a difficult and serious scramble and should only be done in dry conditions. The first two pools are passed on the right, easily at first but with increasing difficulty, as far as the main falls. Difficult climbing up the right wall then leads to a point where the path comes close to the stream. Enter the stream bed and cross it to the left side of the next fall where you confront the major difficulties of the route. Climb a steep corner and descend a sloping ledge to gain the right side of the fall. Climb steeply up the right wall and so gain the stream bed before continuing more easily to the end of the difficulties.

From here there are several possibilities. The first is to pick your way up the craggy fellside above Greencove Wyke, which can give a long and open scramble up slabs, many of them quite exposed. There are plenty of options but good route-finding is needed to link the best scrambling and stay at a reasonable standard. Alternatively, having passed Cam Spout you can continue up the main path to Mickledore and climb Broad Stand – a logical and important step in any lakeland lover's progress.

Descent from Scafell can be made southwards to Slight Side, a lovely ramble on a warm summer's evening, with a detour to delightful Stony Tarn. Pale rocks and dark heather make this a magical place in evening light. Even if you stay until the sun sets it is only a short walk down the fell past Reelplace Noddle to the Woolpack Inn and a much-needed pint.

View into Esk Gorge – the final fall

Route 27: TARN BECK, GREAT BLAKE RIGG AND A ROUND OF SEATHWAITE TARN

	1	2	3
grade (Tarn Beck)	*		
grade (Great Blake Rigg)		*	
quality			
navigation			

ASSESSMENT: A thundering gill followed by an open buttress scramble giving access to high fells and a fine round of the Old Man and Dow.

OS MAP: Outdoor Leisure 6
GR: 234984
DISTANCE: 14km (8.5 miles)

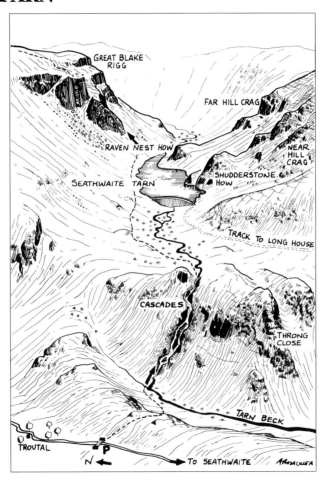

The Duddon is surely the finest river valley in Cumbria. Far from the activity that invades much of the Lakes, it remains unspoilt, undeveloped and relatively unexplored. Even the road south into the Duddon, over Wrynose if you approach from Langdale, is like passing through a time warp into some Himalayan Shangri-La. Wordsworth who loved the place enough to write a fistful of sonnets to the Duddon, would notice few changes, I am sure. Perhaps its lack of that essential tourist ingredient, a ribbon lake, has saved it from ribbon development.

This scramble takes in a round of skyline above Seathwaite Tarn and offers a fine day on the fells with two very enjoyable yet contrasting scrambles. There are several more of equal quality on the rocky outcrops on the approach to the tarn but this combination of Tarn Beck and Great Blake Rigg is the most direct and continuously interesting.

TARN BECK

There are parking places near the cattle grid on the Duddon Road (GR:234984). From here follow a path south across Troutal Tongue towards Worm How and so gain Tarn Beck with its twin streams and foaming cascades. There are plenty of scrambling options but the water

One of the Sheffield lads above Seathwaite Tarn on Great Blake Rigg

level will dictate the driest line.

Above a widening, the stream ahead falls either side of a rock barrier. A rib marked by an obvious rock gendarme should be gained and followed. When the water level is low the left-hand channel provides an interesting, easier alternative.

Continue on northwards with little difficulty and plenty of options, either following the bouldery stream bed or the rocks to the side. Above, the left-hand channel provides the more demanding options but relies on low water. The alternative is slabby scrambling up the side of the right-hand water course. Whichever line you choose, follow it until the streams converge. Ahead, the stream has cut a single cleft. If the water level allows, enter this from the left and scramble up slabs to reach an obvious spur on the left higher up. At this point the scrambling has more or less run out.

GREAT BLAKE RIGG

To continue, gain the main footpath on the left leading to Seathwaite Tarn which in fact provides water for Barrow. The dam is an ugly thing but does not altogether detract from this marvellous place. I am told there are plenty of trout in the lake which, by the number of fishy references on the map, has surely been true in the past. In the 1700s a curate of Seathwaite, one Robert Walker, was allowed to net the tarn for trout once a year to supplement his meagre stipend of £5 per annum. For this sum, apart from his godly work, he was expected to teach the parish children 8 hours a day, 5 days a week.

Follow the sometimes boggy path round the northern shore of the lake and head for the impressive stepped buttresses of Great Blake Rigg. This lies at the head of the Seathwaite Tarn at the foot of Grey Friar (GR:259995). The base of the crag is marked by black overhangs. Climb up to the base of the crag and begin the scramble to the right of the overhangs by following a deep and obvious crack line; this is not altogether simple but quickly leads to a rock platform. Easier ground follows, leading to a steep wall. Zigzag first right then left to reach gentler ground and at a point level with the overhangs on the left. A slab then leads right to the top of the first step in the buttress. Most of these difficulties can be avoided on the right by following a line of grassy ramps and small rock steps.

A second slabby step in the crag is easily gained by a traverse to the right. Climb up easy rock on the left, bypassing a grassy hollow to reach a steeper step. A ledge line leads right, giving access to slabs and good scrambling to the top of this buttress with wonderful views over the tarn.

Now move back left to broken slabs which can be climbed to an obvious ledge. Vegetative rock on the left leads towards the final step marked by an obvious steep corner. Climb a groove right of this corner in an exposed position to gain a rib on the right and the top of the scramble.

To complete the round continue over Grey Friar and descend rough ground between Black Spouts and Fairfield before following a well marked traversing path that slowly climbs south to Swirl Band and Levers Hawse. From here a path descends back to Seathwaite Tarn, but a better day out is to continue to The Old Man of Coniston before backtracking a little to Goat's Hawse and making the climb to the top of Dow. From this wonderful look-out the route continues over Buck and Brown Pike to gain the Walna Scar Road westwards. If you fancied it, you could always descend to the foot of Dow where there are several scrambles on offer.

Now all that remains is to descend through the quarry workings, the oldest in the lakes, as far as Long House. From here leave the 'road', taking the path to Tongue House where a footbridge leads back to Troutal Tongue and the cattle grid.

Route 28: MAIN FACE PIKE O' STICKLE AND THE LANGDALE SKYLINE

	1	2	3
grade			
quality			
navigation			

ASSESSMENT: An intricate scramble on a high, exposed mountain buttress; well worth the effort of gaining the first rocks.

GR: 286062, Old Dungeon Ghyll Hotel
OS MAP: Outdoor Leisure 6
DISTANCE: 16km (10 miles) with multiple ascents and descents

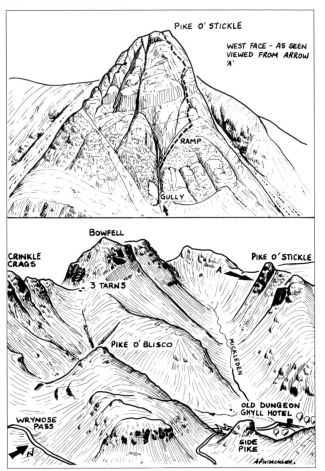

PIKE O' STICKLE
WEST FACE - AS SEEN VIEWED FROM ARROW 'A'
RAMP
GULLY

BOWFELL
PIKE O' STICKLE
CRINKLE CRAGS
3 TARNS
PIKE O' BLISCO
MICKLEDEN
WRYNOSE PASS
N
OLD DUNGEON GHYLL HOTEL
SIDE PIKE
A.PHIZACKLEA

There is something exciting about scrambling on Pike o'Stickle that has a lot to do with its shape, the most easily recognisable in the Lake District. Stickle is a pointed, barrel-chested peak rising steeply from the deep, glaciated trench of Mickleden. It is always exciting to find a relatively easy and exposed way up improbable-looking ground and the main face of Pike o' Stickle certainly provides that.

Shape and ruggedness are only part of the fascination of the Pike; its ancient history is also a draw. The massive main face of Pike o' Stickle is defined between two scree shoots, with the lowest rocks forming Stickle Breast. The right-hand is a true gully, forming a narrow cleft between rocky walls. High in this gully on the rocky flank of the Pike a square-cut cave is clearly visible. Only small, it was once a Neolithic workshop where an artisan worked stone axes and arrow heads. It seems remarkable that our primitive ancestor should have discovered such a remote source of essential material. If you search diligently you can still find fragments chipped from these early tools. It is even more fascinating to think that they were traded elsewhere, both inside and outside the district, 2000 years before Christ, along routeways we still tread. Indeed, it is obvious that the Romans, during their occupation, followed and sometimes improved existing lines of communication throughout the Lakes. Even High Street, the

route over the fells which is often credited as being a Roman road, was well established long before the legions built their wall to the north.

The Old Dungeon Ghyll forms the natural starting point for climbing on the Pike. A rocky path behind the hotel leads up Mickleden (part of the Cumbria Way) far below the Pikes. A gate marks the end of the walled outfields at Grave Gill and a faint trod leads diagonally across Langdale Fell towards Stickle Breast. Be careful not to take the more direct line towards Gimmer Crag where there is plenty of rock but all a bit too serious for scrambling. An alternative, perhaps better, approach is to continue along the main path to Troughton Beck where another path leads well left of the crag, from where it is possible to cross a scree shoot to gain a terrace which leads to the start of the scramble. Whichever approach you choose, the ascent is steep. The objective is a terrace crossed by a path above the broken crags guarding the lowest part of the main face.

The right side of the main face is cut by an obvious grass-filled gully which provides the start of the scramble. Follow its rocky bed which finds a way through the first barrier of loose, grassy rocks and leads to better things on the upper main face.

Difficulties in the gully can be avoided on the right. Beyond a widening in the gully a path enters from the left and exits right along

The Langdale Pikes with the great scree shoot of Stickle defining the scramble up its main face

a heathery terrace. Follow this to below the rocks of the main face which is marked by a cracked steep wall. Avoid this wall on the right where easier rock leads up a nose to a terrace above the cracks. Beyond this, leftwards, reach another terrace and follow this to the right where there is an obvious slabby weakness. Climb the slabs, keeping left of an overhang to reach a flat-topped rock.

Above is a well marked band of Grey Rock. Go right for about half a rope's length and climb steeply up sound rock to reach the top of the Grey Band. Now scramble diagonally leftwards over slabby rock to reach a prominent, leaning block. Scramble up right of this to reach easier ground, leading rightwards to easy-angled slabs which can be followed to the top of the Pike.

Having gained this volcanic plug-like peak there is a choice of rounds. North-west you can cross Martcrag Moor and Stake Gill to traverse Black Crags and gain Rossett Pike. A good day would continue south-west to Ore Gap and take in Bow Fell, Three Tarns, Crinkle Crags and Cold Pike. From this last top a footpath descends to shallow Red Tarn where there is a decision to be made. Either descend north down Browney Gill which offers some easy scrambling in its lower half, and return to the Old Dungeon Gill by way of Oxendale. Or, if time and legs allow, scramble up craggy Pike o' Blisco and follow the path leading beside Redacre Gill to the road and Wall End Barn, once famous as a climbers' doss.

Of course, if you do not fancy a round of the

Langdale skyline but are looking for more scrambling, turn from the summit of Pike o' Stickle and follow the path east towards Harrison Stickle as far as the top of Dungeon Ghyll. Descend towards Thorn Crag and the south-west face of Harrison which provides a delightful scramble (p.124).

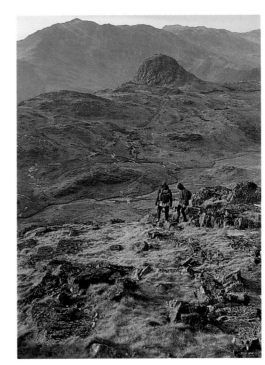

The biscuit-barrel summit of Pike o' Stickle from Harrison Stickle

Route 29: DUNGEON GHYLL, HARRISON STICKLE AND JACK'S RAKE

	1	2	3
grade (Dungeon Gill lower)			
grade (Dungeon Gill upper)			
grade (Harrison Stickle)			
grade (Jack's Rake)			
quality			
navigation			

ASSESSMENT: A classic scramble up one of the most famous ghylls in the Lake District, followed by exposed scrambling to the summit of Harrison Stickle.

OS MAP: Outdoor Leisure 6
GR: 296064, New Dungeon Ghyll Hotel
DISTANCE: 5km (3.1 miles); short and sharp, but still a fine day

To climb the Pikes by way of DungeonGhyll provides the scrambler with a continuously interesting route to the tops. Apart from a short initial walk the way up the gill is nearly always interesting. Even when the scrambling runs out, the scenery is superb and the anticipation of what is in store is exciting. Descending Pavey by way of Jack's Rake is a great way of finishing the round, but finding its start is difficult in anything but good visibility.

From the the New Dungeon Ghyll Hotel, follow the track towards Stickle Ghyll until a path soon breaks out left following a boundary wall leading in the direction of Dungeon Ghyll, cutting deeply into the hillside. Go through the gate and follow the path on the right to a stile and the start of the gill that, for centuries, has served as a natural wonder and tourist attraction – but don't be put off!

The lower gill provides easy but interesting scrambling that initially is little more than walking. But follow the stream to the first hidden waterfall, a superb cascade tumbling 18m (60ft) with a huge jammed boulder forming a natural bridge over the gorge. William Wordsworth undoubtedly knew the place well and used it to good effect in his poem 'The Idle Shepherd Boys'.

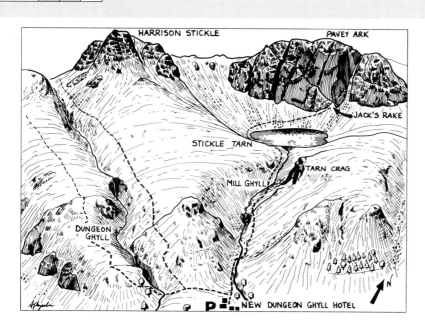

Pavey Ark with identifiable ramp of Jack's Rake slashing across the cliffs

…They leapt – they ran – and when they came Right opposite to Dungeon-Ghyll,
…'Cross, if you dare, where I shall cross –
Come on, and tread where I shall tread.'
The other took him at his word,
And followed as he led.
It was a spot which you may see
If ever you to Langdale go;
Into a chasm a mighty block
Hath fallen, and made a bridge of rock:
The gulf is deep below;
And, in a basin black and small,
Receives a lofty waterfall.

Having explored the scene, and crossed if you dare, retrace your steps and climb out of the ravine to gain the main path that climbs left of the stream. You can re-enter the stream bed but not too soon as there are a couple of unclimbable falls. Difficulty will depend on the water level, but in any case the problems can be avoided by rejoining the walkers' path.

Ahead there is another large fall at the head of a bay. Climb this steeply on the left and continue up the stream bed through a field of huge boulders which leads in turn to another fine but unclimbable cascade. Circumvent this via a gully on the left which is loose in places but leads quite easily to open ground and fine views of Harrison Stickle. Ruskin wrote of this lower section, 'the loveliest rock scenery, chased with silver waterfalls, that I ever set foot or heart upon'.

The narrow upper ravine provides one

difficult pitch which cannot be avoided. Enter the narrow gorge, crossing boulders of red rough rock to reach a large fall. It can only be passed by a steep, rocky gully on the right. Traverse to it from the left to gain the foot of a steep groove. Ascend this on good holds and continue up the wider chimney as far as a chockstone. Climb this with difficulty and continue more easily to the top of the scrambling. Above and to the right is a small pinnacle beside the footpath below the impressive south-west flank of Harrison Stickle. This marks the start of the next scramble, forming a natural and continuous route to the summit. It is possible to exit from the chimney before the chockstone by a traverse line on the left which regains the stream bed above the fall. You can then continue up the gill without much difficulty and traverse back on the footpath to the pinnacle.

From the small detached pinnacle move up on the right over grass to the foot of a rock groove. Climb this on good holds and so gain another grassy area above. Trend diagonally right to gain what appears to be a rock rib. Climb onto this and continue diagonally rightwards on good holds and in a fine position. The choice of routes is endless but the aim is to connect as many good pieces of climbable rock as possible. In fact, superb rough rock

Harrison Stickle above Stickle Gill on a fine autumn day

steps and slabs lead to the very summit of the mounain; a delightful scramble.

Harrison Stickle is a fine viewpoint and whilst you are on top you might want to stay high and take in the Pike. However, a great way of finishing the round is to traverse towards Pavey and descend by way of Jack's Rake. Like all the best scrambles, the route is highly improbable. The rocky ramp that forms the rack cuts an easy but exposed line across a steep cliff. In all but good visibility, finding it from above is the main problem. Several cairns lead to a well trodden path that descends to the top of the Rake which is exposed. Once discovered, the way ahead is obvious. The Rake itself follows a fault line which, in wet conditions, is a drainage trough and slippery. The scrambling is nowhere difficult and the way is obvious and follows rock continuously in an impressive position. At the bottom of the Rake, descend the scree to Stickle Tarn. During the middle of the last century this superbly positioned glacial tarn was dammed to provide an emergency water supply for the gunpowder works at Elterwater. The explosives were essential for the local slate industry. A footpath runs round the tarn to the dam where a well used path descends steeply from this hanging cwm to the New Dungeon Ghyll Hotel.

A bird's eye view of Harrison Stickle, Stickle Tarn and half-hidden Pavey Ark

Route 30: GREAT CARRS BUTTRESS WITH SWIRL HOW AND WETHERLAM OR TILBERTHWAITE GILL

	1	2	3
grade (Great Carrs Buttress)			
grade (Tilberthwaite Gill)	*		
quality			
navigation			

ASSESSMENT: A fine, open buttress scramble followed by a ridge walk to Wetherlam and a rocky descent to Tilberthwaite Gill.

OS MAP: Outdoor Leisure 6
GR: 316033, limited parking around Little Langdale
DISTANCE: 13km (8.1 miles)

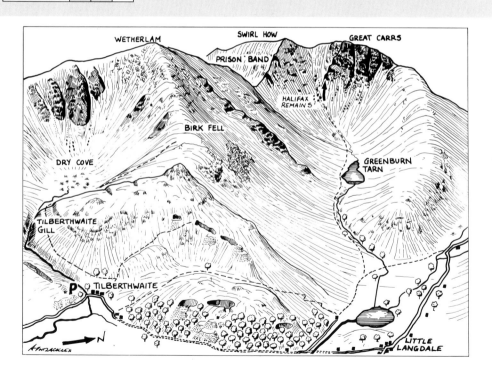

Wrynose Pass has always proven a hard crossing. After Agricola's legionaries built their forts on the Hardknott and Wrynose, the Norsemen laid claim to the Esk, Duddon and Langdale Valleys. Settling inland from the fine natural harbour of Ravenglass and the Furness ports, the valleys of Cumbria must have seemed a 'home far from home'.

Little Langdale has long been important for minerals. The fells around it are rich in copper and slate that have been mined for hundreds of years. It was an area central to the Norsemen who were farming these fells before the Normans came. How important it was we can only guess from the archaeological evidence. Behind Fell Foot Farm near Castle Howe there is a terraced mound of stone and earth that stood as a *thingvellir* or parliament, evidence of a burgeoning democracy and strength of character that withstood the Norman onslaught. Statesmen they became, never tenants of the crown but owning their own homes and land, and proud of their independence.

Wetherlam, which seems to have drawn its name from a wether or castrated ram, is the fell which dominates the view from the tarn at Little Langdale. It marks the northern limit of the Coniston Fells and offers fine walking and scrambling. From the summit, a western ridge

Nearing the top of Great Carrs with Little Langdale in the distance

sweeps to Swirl How before swinging north to the crenellated crest of Great and Little Carrs, and finally to Hell Gill Pike and Wet Side Edge. This semicircle of craggy mountains forms the catchment of Greenburn Beck which flows into Little Langdale Tarn, and provides the meat of this enjoyable scramble and round.

GREAT CARRS BUTTRESS

From the pub in Little Langdale cross the Brathay by humpbacked Slater Bridge and follow the path south-west alongside Greenburn Beck. For centuries the northern slopes of Wetherlam have been mined for slate and copper. In particular, those above Greenburn Beck were rich in copper and were once worked to within a stone's throw of the summit.

Although the beck does not provide much scrambling, the course it has cut is very lovely; a myriad of pools and small cascades flowing over potted and polished green slate. Follow the path past workings and old shafts to a reservoir enlarged from a small tarn to serve the needs of mining. All are witness to the frenetic industry these hills once held. Beyond the reservoir you enter a deep mountain combe rising steeply to the top of Broad Slack, to the right of which are the broken crags of Great Carrs.

Climb steadily up the fellside, making for the base of Great Carrs Buttress, keeping an eye out for remnants of a Halifax bomber that crashed on the return leg of a raid on Berlin in 1944. Its engines sit in the stream bed. Scramble up the initial rocks, or avoid them on the left. The rocks now steepen and are capped by a perched boulder (GR:274011). Above it the face is not too steep or continuous but is made up of rough rock broken by vegetation that can be climbed almost anywhere. Climb to the block and continue up the stepped ridge above, making the best of the climbable rock before the angle eases towards the upper crag. There are lots of possible route choices from here; the best is on the right up a rock rib before the gully. Although quite steep the holds are good and by linking the best of the rock it is possible to make a scramble almost to the summit.

If the aim is to make a short day of it, descend over Hell Gill Pike and Wet Side Edge by a path leading down to Greenburn Beck. Alternatively, make a longer round by following the ridge, past the cross to the RAF crew and on to Swirl How down Prison Band to Wetherlam. The route down Wetherlam Edge is enjoyable enough but better still is to follow the mountain's southern ridge above Hen Crag and Lower Hows to the small tarn at the head of Steel Edge.

TILBERTHWAITE GILL

Descend steeply down the rocky edge north-east to Dry Cove Bottom and the head of Tilberthwaite Gill, forming the upper part of Yewdale Beck. In Victorian times this was a scenic walkway, with bridges and rails to make things easy. Today they are gone, but thankfully this lovely, deep-cut gill remains to provide an interesting scramble in either direction. Of course, with water raging through its narrow ravine it is both impossible and dangerous and should be avoided.

There is a choice of routes back to Little Langdale. The most direct is to follow the mine track from High Tilberthwaite through the quarries to Atkinson Coppice and return to Slater Bridge. If time allows, Hodge Close Quarries are worth exploring. Vast caverns and pits have been formed where the miners have taken away the slate, leaving an impressive monument to their labour and the past importance of their product. Although the slate is still worked on a small scale, the quarries have found a new life. Divers explore the waters and climbers have bolted many of the steep, blank walls of smooth, green slate.

Looking up the sweep of Great Carrs from Swirl How

Route 31: LOW WATER BECK, BRIM FELL AND CONISTON FELLS

	1	2	3
grade (Low Water Beck)			
grade (Brim Fell)			
quality			
navigation			

ASSESSMENT: Two scrambles that gain a height of over 430m (1419ft) through impressive scenery in an area rich in history.

GR: 289971, parking by the moor gate/Walna Scar Road
OS MAP: Outdoor Leisure 6
DISTANCE: 12km (7.5 miles)
A delightful round

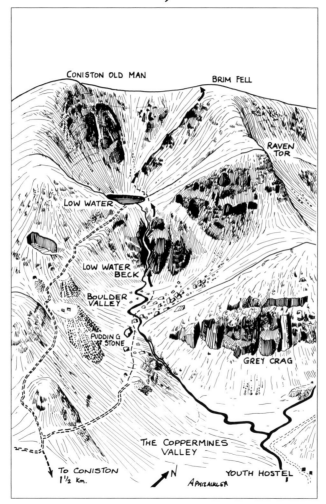

CONISTON OLD MAN
BRIM FELL
RAVEN TOR
LOW WATER
LOW WATER BECK
BOULDER VALLEY
PUDDING STONE
GREY CRAG
THE COPPERMINES VALLEY
TO CONISTON 1½ Km.
N
YOUTH HOSTEL
A PRIZACKLER

History is piled layer upon layer around Coniston. Here even the geology is complicated, with the Borrowdale volcanics bordering warm-water limestone, with slate and fine grits bound in succession, all telling the most ancient story. Between the Old Man and Wetherlam the fells carry the deep scars of glaciation, with rounded, sheep-backed rocks gouged as if by some icy predator. Scattered boulders and moraine mounds are piled like monstrous spoilheaps excavated from hollow combes, saucering cold, clear tarns.

On top of this solid geological history a more transient story has been told, the most obvious of which is mining. But a close look at the map shows that long before the Romans and Vikings settled in the area ancient Britons left their mark. Stone circles, enclosures, homesteads and cairns litter the place. The museum in Coniston holds a burial urn taken from a Neolithic stone circle unearthed on Banniside above Torver. Over 2,000 years old, it holds the ashes, teeth and a few treasures of a mother and child. In more recent times, Agricola's legionaries worked the hills for copper and lead and, in the early Elizabethan period, under the direction of German engineers, the Company of Mines Royal successfully dug the fells here and elsewhere in Cumbria. The copper deposits were rich and provided the livelihood for hundreds of men, as did slate during the second half of the last century. Today, all that is left are the spoils of a battle lost in a war. Nature is winning ultimately, although one level is still

being worked at the head of Coppermines Valley. This amount of historical interest to the area makes a day on the fells even more fascinating.

LOW WATER BECK

Of all the high tarns around the Old Man, Low Water is the most profound. Backed by a semicircle of high crags, the water stands in a dish of solid volcanic rock. A few years ago I flew from the summit of the Old Man and circled the tarn, my canopy flexing on the thermals and turbulence off Brim Fell. The dark waters had a hypnotic pull so I turned from the shadowy mountain to follow the beck into sunshine and then above the old mine track. Flying close to Stubthwaite Crag searching for lift, I circled the walled fields at the start of the Walna Scar Road before landing alongside a party of picnickers near the moor gate!

On foot it takes longer but the sensation can be equally intense. I must thank Harry Griffin for pointing out this combination of Low Water Beck and Brim Fell, a long scramble to the fell tops. From the start of the Walna Scar Road above Coniston, a miner's track snakes in the direction of Levers Water on a hillside littered with levels, holes and workings. Follow the track between Stubthwaite Crag and The Bell to Crowberry Haws where the track to the Old

Steep, open scrambling on Brim Fell above sparkling Low Water

Man goes left, steeply up the hillside. Continue straight on at the same level amongst quarry workings to reach Low Water Beck and an area of massive boulders. Dumped by the glaciers in a trench known as Boulder Valley, many are named and provide good sport. The largest of the blocks is called the Pudding Stone which, in the past, was a favourite 'climbing wall' for lakeland tigers. A circuit of this boulder's problems will certainly warm you up for the scramble ahead.

Beyond the Pudding Stone, Low Water Beck falls down a steep crag in a number of impressive cascades. Our route stays on the right of the falls, climbing water-washed rock and following the most enjoyable line of resistance. Scramble up the deep-cut slit to the foot of the first obstacle, where the only escape is steeply out right, to gain a comfortable ledge above a precipice. Follow the obvious ramp right to a terrace below a rock barrier. The most interesting scrambling avoids this by an exposed traverse left where a bold step onto a jammed block lets you gain slabs and a heathery shelf. Continue to the top of the cascade by scrambling more easily up slabs by the edge of the stream at the end of the first steep section.

Now the way lies over boulders, followed to a point where the stream divides around a steep step which can be climbed by a ramp.

At the start of Low Water Beck where high water always means a soaking

Go left to climb a vegetative groove to reach another slab above the impassable deep cleft cut by Low Water Beck. The exposed edge of the slab on the left provides a fine finish to the beck on fine holds and with good friction in dry conditions.

BRIM FELL

Low Water sits in an impressive hollow, shadowy and often brooding, overflown only by ravens and the odd paraglider. In winter, the slopes right of the zigzagging track leading to the Old Man provide interesting climbing, but not in summer. By far the best route to the tops is an ascent of Brim Fell to the north. Easier than the beck, it is much more in keeping and makes the most of the rough volcanic rock that makes Coniston's crags so good to climb on.

Walk around the tarn to its west side to where an obvious spur rises from a stream to a rock slab. Gain the slabs and climb them on the left. A steeper section follows with more slabs to the right. Above these and further right still there is a rib leading to more accommodating slabs or rough rock leading to a buttress which is climbed to a point where a gully on the left can be reached. Climb this until better ground on the right wall leads you close to the summit. The rock is wonderful to climb on throughout this area, being rough and well laden with incut holds. Take care, however, as in places it is shattered and holds flake off alarmingly.

The fells are now your oyster. The Old Man is but a stride away whilst the ridge to Swirl

How and Wetherlam beckons in the opposite direction. The walk along the top is the very best, offering fine views towards the sea, Seathwaite Tarn and, of course, the Esk side of Scafell. If you choose this route you could return over the Furness Fells and explore Coppermines Valley.

If you are looking for more scrambling Dow Crag (p.136) can be reached quickly via Goat's

Walking on water in Low Water Beck near the top of the first section

Hawse or, if you prefer the walk to Wetherlam, you can easily traverse into Great Carrs Buttress from Swirl Hawse for another delightful scramble. Alternatively you could descend the north-eastern spur of Brim Fell down Raven Tor to Levers Water for a route on Great How.

Route 32: DOW: F BUTTRESS AND B BUTTRESS

	1	2	3
grade (F Buttress)			*
grade (B Buttress)			*
quality			
navigation			

ASSESSMENT: Two exposed scrambles on a major cliff that provide exhilarating situations. Easily incorporated in a round of the Coniston Fells or added to a scramble up Low Water and Brim Fell.

OS MAP: Outdoor Leisure 6 **GR:**289970 Coniston, or from the Duddon Valley **DISTANCE:** 10km (6.2 miles) Easily extended to take in the Old Man and other fells

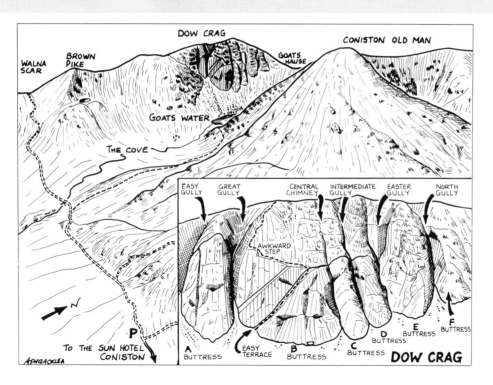

$\mathcal{D}$ow Crag is a real gem of a cliff for rock climbers but it did not really inspire the first wave of cragsmen. Perhaps it was too far from Wasdale and the really high mountains or perhaps it was the nearness of all the old mining industry and Coniston where Ruskin lived and keenly criticised their 'greased pole' antics. As it was, they came, explored a little, then left for higher things on Scafell and Pillar. It needed a later generation, after the First World War, to fill blanks on the steeper buttresses and to realise the real worth of Dow. Despite the fierce look of the place, Dow does have a few gems to detain the scrambler in search of steep ground and interesting route-finding.

Whether you are in the Duddon Valley or Coniston the best approach to Dow is the same – take the Walna Scar Road. An alternative from the Duddon is to scramble up to Seathwaite Tarn, cross Goat's Hawse and traverse into the foot of the crag. In the same way it can complete a day spent scrambling up Low Water Beck and Brim Fell (p.132) from where an easy descent also leads to Goat's Hawse.

The scarred fells above Coniston have been worked for centuries, leaving behind a honeycomb of levels, spoilheaps, rotting workings and much of interest concerning our recent past. I quite enjoy wandering about the old workings and exploring the levels, now that they are being reclaimed by the

Dow Crag seen from high above the Old Man

mountain. The spoils give meaning to the layers of history that make the Lake District's landscape what it is. On the other hand, I like it as it is and would be outraged if the National Park allowed RTZ or some other multi-national to rip the heart out of a fellside and leave a modern mess.

Of the Dow scrambles, and there are surprisingly few, my favourites are the spur of F Buttress and well known Easy Terrace which zigzags up B Buttress right of Great Gully. Because of the nature of the ground, all scrambles on Dow are serious and exposed and are only recommended to those with rock-climbing experience and skills.

F Buttress

F Buttress is the most northerly of Dow's buttresses, separated from E Buttress by the deep cleft of North Gully. It forms a narrow triangle of broken, vegetative rock with a well defined spur rising to the summit rocks; this provides the line of the scramble. Begin well right of North Gully where the spur of F emerges from a smaller gully. Climb this spur to a ledge below a rock wall. Keeping close to the gully, climb this until blocked by steeper ground. Descend left down a grassy terrace to a grass-filled crack that finds a way through the difficulty. Continue up a groove leading into a chimney. The exit from this is out to the

F Buttress separated from E Buttress by the deep cleft of North Gully

left where the ridge and easier ground can be reached. An easier scramble from the base of the buttress can be had by following the gully.

Dow's first pioneers must have been impressed by its steep buttresses. The first route was on E Buttress, climbed by the 'prince of pioneers', Walter Parry Haskett-Smith in 1886. More famous for his ascent of Napes Needle, he was followed by others often listed in the *dramatis personae* of lakeland exploration: Slingsby, Hastings, Jones (the Only Genuine) and the Keswick brothers, George and Ashley Abraham.

B Buttress

Over on B Buttress, which has a Mountain Rescue stretcher box at its base, there is another well used scramble – Easy Terrace. This follows the well marked diagonal rock ramp that rises across the wide, rounded pillar of B from near the base of Great Gully. This rake begins in a shallow gully and ends half way up the pillar at a horizontal ledge that runs across the buttress. The whole, both ramp and ledge, form Easy Terrace. Scrambling up the rake is straight-forward and leads to the horizontal terrace without route-finding difficulty. Do not follow this terrace to the right but break out to the left by scrambling up a series of ledges, finding the best line of least resistance. This is often used by climbers in descent so care should be taken to avoid stonefall. The route is exposed through-out but leads steeply to the summit of the crag where a narrow ridge leads to the summit of Dow.

Route 33: BELLES KNOTT, THE EASEDALE MATTERHORN, BY WAY OF SOURMILK AND EASEDALE GILLS

	1	2	3
grade (Sourmilk Gill)			
grade (Easedale Gill)			
grade (Belles Knott)			
quality			
navigation			

ASSESSMENT: A delightful round that avoids the well worn paths amongst some of the districts most popular fells.

GR: 328083, limited parking on lane leading to Easedale Tarn; plenty of parking in Grasmere
DISTANCE: 10km (6.2 miles)

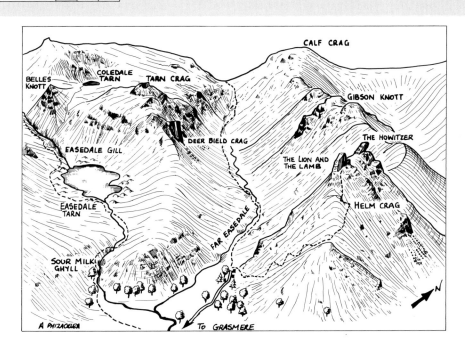

If ever the villages of the Lake District are twinned with a European counterpart, Grasmere will surely find its *doppelgänger* in Zermatt. There are endless comparisons. The fame and name of Zermatt grew because of artist, writer and mountaineer Edward Whymper. His ascent of the Matterhorn in 1865 brought an end to the Golden Age of Alpine mountaineering and gave everlasting prosperity to Zermatt, where cash tills have long replaced cow-bells and summer cheese-making.

As Whymper is to Zermatt so Wordsworth is to Grasmere. Visitors flock to the place to pay homage to the poet and wander beside its lake, beneath its trees in search of souvenirs and endless cream teas. It is not only the 'wordsmith' that has brought Grasmere recognition; the multi-talented Heaton-Cooper family have for generations been the quintessential water-colourists of the district and in turn attract the tourist to their lovely studio in the village. I have no wish to put either place down – both are charming in their way and have much to offer – but both should be avoided at the height of the holiday season.

My comparison does not end with neat streets and cream teas, however. Whymper was attracted to Zermatt because of the Matterhorn and, after his tragic ascent, wrote *Scrambles Amongst The Alps* 1860–69. Grasmere has its own mini Matterhorn, which is the subject of this chapter (given just a little licence) – and I

don't mean Helm Crag. It provides a really enjoyable scramble amongst some lovely scenery and takes in both a fine summit and a good ridge; not bad for a day that can be comfortably completed within 6 hours.

One of the most popular walks from Grasmere is up the well marked path to Easedale. In a way, the tarn is like the Schwartzsee below the Matterhorn, without the reastaurants – although even Easedale in the past boasted a hut selling refreshments. But where, you may wonder, is Easedale's Matterhorn? It is to be found in an ascent of the south-east ridge of Belles Knott which, when viewed from the approach up slabby Easedale Gill, forms an impressive triangle of rock not wholly unlike the Matterhorn – if looked at with a poet's eye.

SOURMILK GILL

The round begins by following the tourist track leading towards Easedale Tarn. Ahead the well worn track rises to the left of a cascading Sourmilk Gill which provides the line for the first of the day's scrambling. There is nothing difficult about the route-finding or the climbing. Simply follow the best way up the rocky stream bed as dictated by the level of the water, or wind your way up the slabby steps on the left side of the stream. It is certainly much more enjoyable than wandering up the path, which you must finally join beyond a steep step above an obvious plungepool.

The tarn is a delightful place, described by Wordsworth's friend, de Quincey, as, 'A chapel within a cathedral – a little private oratory within a chapel'. Full of fish, it attracts all manner of waterbirds, including grebe and cormorant. It also provides a mirror with which to reflect distant Dollywagon Pike and Fairfield perfectly. But turn your back on that view and follow the path meandering around the lake towards Easedale Gill and look instead at the attractive rocky outcrop of Belles Knott – Easedale's Matterhorn.

EASEDALE GILL AND BELLES KNOTT

Scrambling on the second leg of the day follows the exposed rocks of Easedale Gill, rising steeply from boggy ground beyond the moraine-dammed tarn. Once again, the scrambling is straight-forward; an obvious water-worn slab is followed by steeper steps in the stream bed. Always on good, clean rock, always escapable but thoroughly enjoyable, the profile of the Knott above becomes increasingly impressive, like the Matterhorn from the Hornli Hut.

The ascent of the Knott is made up the right-hand skyline ridge. By leaving the gill at the top of the scrambling you can traverse rightwards to the foot of the lowest rocks where a cluster of juniper and the weather-bleached remains of a rowan indicate the start. The arête just to the right of a dead tree provides the best line up an edge of rough rock and leads to a grassy ramp. Follow the ramp leftwards, where a steeper step on good holds leads more or less up the edge with increasing exposure, even more so if you keep to the left. All too soon the scramble comes to an end on the rocky summit, where unlike the Matterhorn there is an easy way off. Grassy slopes quickly lead back to the main path, but if you have the time it is much more interesting to continue and complete a round of Far Easedale.

The most interesting route leads first to lonely Codale Tarn and then steeply west to Sergeant Man. From there turn north-east to descend between Ash and Ferngill crags and pick up the ridge line that forms the northern boundary of Far Easedale. This delightful and undulating ramble skirts strangely named Pike of Carrs and Gibson Knott, and eventually culminates on the rocky topknot of Helm Crag. This is an impressive place where the Lion and Lamb stand guard and face each other on the summit. There is plenty to delay the scrambler here as the rocks offer fine sport amongst impressive terrain. At the far end of the ridge the path falls steeply to regain the track back to Grasmere and the promise of tea and stickies.

A view to inspire poets: Sourmilk Gill on the approach to Easedale Tarn

ACKNOWLEDGEMENTS

Thanks are due to a great many friends that shared their days on the hill unselfishly, opting for my choice of route, putting up with my photography and my demands to have a look at another line – without them it would not have been possible: Sallie O'Connor, Ronnie Faux, Alan George, Bill and Margaret Freeland, Bruce and Charlotte West, the Sheffield lads, William O'Connor, Mike Parsons and Chris Brasher.

I must also record a debt of thanks to all guidebook writers who laboriously and pains-takingly record the actions of climbers so that we can enjoy and share their discoveries. The early guidebooks of the Fell and Rock Climbers Club have been invaluable. Editors like H.M. Kelly, Bentley Beetham, A.T. Hargreaves, A.R. Thompson, Astley Cooper and E. Wood-Johnston have all provided inspiration and information. More recently, the guidebooks of Brian Evans have become the *Guide Vallot* of Lake District scrambling. Three other authors have always been my bedside reading: over the years, Harry Griffin provided more words on Cumbria than anyone I know, dead or living, a Cumbrian born and bred, he's a real mountaineer; W. Heaton Cooper's book *The Tarns of Lakeland* is an encyclopaedia; and finally Robert Gamble's book of *Place Names* is a real eye opener. My thanks to them all and to others I may have unintentionally failed to acknowledge.

Bill O'Connor
Little Strickland
Cumbria

High over Honister. The Crux pitch on Honister Crag

INDEX

Page numbers in *italic* indicate photographs

Armboth Hall, 25
Arrowhead Ridge, *112*, 113
Ashness Gill, 24–6, *26*
Atkinson, John, 62
Attic Cave, 37

Baumgartner, C.A.O., 62
Beetham, Bentley, 28, 30–31, 34, 36, 37, 38
Bell Rib, Yewbarrow, 101
Belles Knott, 139–41
Bessyboot, 35
Birkness Comb, 49, 50–3
Black Sail Pass, 63, 107, 113
Bleaberry Tarn, 49
Bleawater Crag Gill, 87–9, *88, 89*
Blencathra, *2, 15*, 77–80, *79*
Borrowdale, 27–9, 31, 35, 36
Bowderdale Boulder, 101
Brim Fell, 132, *133*, 135, 136
Broad Stand, 6, *18–19, 21*, 20–2, 104, 117
Brotherilkeld, 102, 116
Browncove Crags, 74–5, *75*
Browny Gill, 123
Buttermere, 45, 47, 49

Catstye Cam, 96
Cam Crag, 38–40, *39, 40*
Cam Spout, 117
Castle Rock, 70–1
Chockstone Ridge, 50, *51–2*, 53
Coledale Hause, 57
Coledale Tarn, 141
Coleridge, Samuel Taylor, 6, 21–2, 104
Combe Gill, 35–7

Coniston museum, 132
Coniston, Old Man, 120, 132, 133, 135
Corridor Route, 104
Crummock, 54, 57
Cumbria (derivation of the name) 79
Cumbria Way (Allerdale Ramble), 29, 123

Dalehead, 28, *44*
Dalehead Pillar, 41, 43–4
Dalton, Millican, 36–7
Deepdale, 66–9, 92
de Quincey, 141
Dibona, Angelo, 24, 25, 28,
Dob Gill, 61
Dodd's, the, 70–3
Dollywagon Pike, 96
Dove Nest Cave, 36, 37, 39
Dow Crag, 120, 136–8, *137, 138*
Duddon Valley, 118
Dungeon Ghyll, 124–6
Dunmail Raise, 75–6

Eagle Nest Gully, *111,* 113
Easedale Gill, 139–40
Easy Way, the, 62, 64
Elmhow, zig-zags, 92
Ennerdale, 49, 107
Eskdale, 102, 103, 114, 117
Esk Gorge, 114–17, *117*
Esk Hause, 102, 103, 104, 114

Fairfield, 66–9
Faux, Ronnie, 103
Fell Foot Farm, 128
Fleetwith Pike, 45, 47, 51
Gillercomb, 30–4

Gilpin, William, 27
Glaramara, 40
Goldscope mine, 28, 29, 41–3
grading, 16–18
Grains Gill, 103
graphite, 33–4
Grasmere, 139, 141
Grasmoor, 54–7
Great Blake Rigg, 118–20, *119*
Great Carrs Buttress, *129, 131*, 128–32, 135
Great Gable, 30–4, 108–13
Great Moss, 102, 114, 117, *115*
Greenhow End, 66, *67*, 69
Grey Crag, 50–3
Griffin, Harry, 66, 133
Grisedale, 96

Hall's Fell, *13*, 77–80
Harrison Stickle, 123, 124–7, *126, 127*
Harrop Tarn, 61
Harrow Buttress, 50–3
Haskett–Smith, Walter Parry, 6, 90, 98, 109, 113
Haweswater, 84, 87–9
Hay Stacks, 47, *48*, 51, 53
Heaton–Cooper, 139
Helm Crag, 7, 141
Helvellyn, 74, 94–6
Helvellyn Gill, *14*, 74–5, *76*
High Level Route, 63
High Seat, 25, 26
High Stile, 47, 50
High Street, 87–9, 121, *86*
Honister Crag, 45–9, *46, 142*
Hopgill Beck, 84–6, *85*
Hopgill Head, 54–7

Ill Crag, 102–4, *103, 104*
Ill Gill, Kirkfell, *8,* 105–7, *106, 107*
Innominate Tarn, 49, 53
Intake Ridge, *36,* 37
Iron Crag, Middle Fell, 100

Jack's Rake, 124, *125,* 127

Kern Knotts, 110
King Arthur, 70–1
Kirk Fell, 105–7, 113

Langdale, 120–3
Langstrath, 38–40
Lanthwaite Green, 54, 57
Launchy Gill, 58, *59, 61*
Levers Water, 135
Lingcove Bridge, 102, 114
Link Cove Gill, 66–9, *68*
Little Narrowcove, 102, 114
Long Stile Ridge, *86,* 87, 89
Lorton Gully, 54–7
Low Water Beck, 132–4, *134, 135,* 136
Low Water Tarn, 133, *133*

Maiden Moor 27, 28, 43
Manchester, water supply, 25–6, 58, 71, 81
Mardale, 84–6
Mickleden, 122, 123
Mickledore, 20, 22, 104, 117
Mill Gill, *11–12,* 70–3, *71, 72*
mining, 41–3, 132, 136–7
Mosedale (Wasdale), 63, 106
Mosedale Beck (Swindale), 81–3, *82, 83*
Moses (Rigg, Trod), 34, 110, 113
Mummery, A.F., 30

Napes Needle, 6, 34, 109–11, *109*

Nether Beck Gorge, *99, 101,* 100–1, 107
Nethermost, 92, 96
Newlands, 28, 41, *42,* 43
New Dungeon Ghyll, 124, 127
Nitting Haws, *22, 29,* 27–9

Old Corpse Road, 82, 83, 85, 86
Old Dungeon Ghyll, 123
Ore Gap, 123

Patterdale, 66, *91,* 92, 96
Pavey Ark, 124, *125, 127*
Peascod, Bill, 50
Pike o' Stickle, 121–3, *122, 123*
Pillar Rock, 62–4, 107
Pinnacle Ridge, 90–2, *93*
Potter, Beatrix, 27, 41
Pudding Stone, 134

Rabbit's Trod, 34
Red Pike, 49, 53
Red Tarn, Helvellyn, 96
Robinson, John Wilson, 63, 109
Rossett Pike, 123
Rowantreethwaite Gill, 84–6

Saddleback, *see* Blencathra
Sampson's Stones, 117
Scafell, 20–2, 104, *116,* 117
Scafell Pike, 102–4, *115*
Scales Tarn, *78*
Scarth Gap, 53, 63
scrambling, clothing and equipment, 10–12
  definition, 6, 9, 50–1
Seathwaite (Borrowdale), 31, 103, 104
Seathwaite Tarn, 118–19, *119,* 136
Sergeant Man, 141

Sharp Edge, 77–80, *78, 80*
Shipton, Eric, 103
Slab and Notch, 62–4, *63, 64*
Slater Bridge, 129, 130
Sourmilk Gill (Borrowdale) *31, 33,* 30–4
Sourmilk Gill (Grasmere), *140,* 141
Stickle Tarn, 127, *127*
St John's in the Vale, 70–3
Striding Edge, *1, 95,* 94–6
St Sunday Crag, 90–2
Sty Head, 104, 110
Swindale, 81–3
Swirl How, 130, 135
Swirral Edge, 94–6

Tarn Beck, 118–20
The Old West, 62
thingvellir, 128
Thirlmere, 58–61, 74
Thompson, Archer, 24, 28
Tilberthwaite Gill, 130
Truss Gap, 81, 82, 83

Ullscarf, 26, 61

Wainwright, Alfred (AW), 49, 53
Walker, Robert, 120
Walna Scar Road, 120, 133, 136
Wasdale, *11, 97,* 98–101, 105
Watendlath, 25, 26, 61
Westmorland Crag, 113
Wetherlam, 130, 135
Whymper, Edward, 9, 18, 139
Whiteside, 54, *55, 56,* 57
Wordsworth, William, 6, 96, 118, 124–5, 139

Yewbarrow, 99, 101, 107